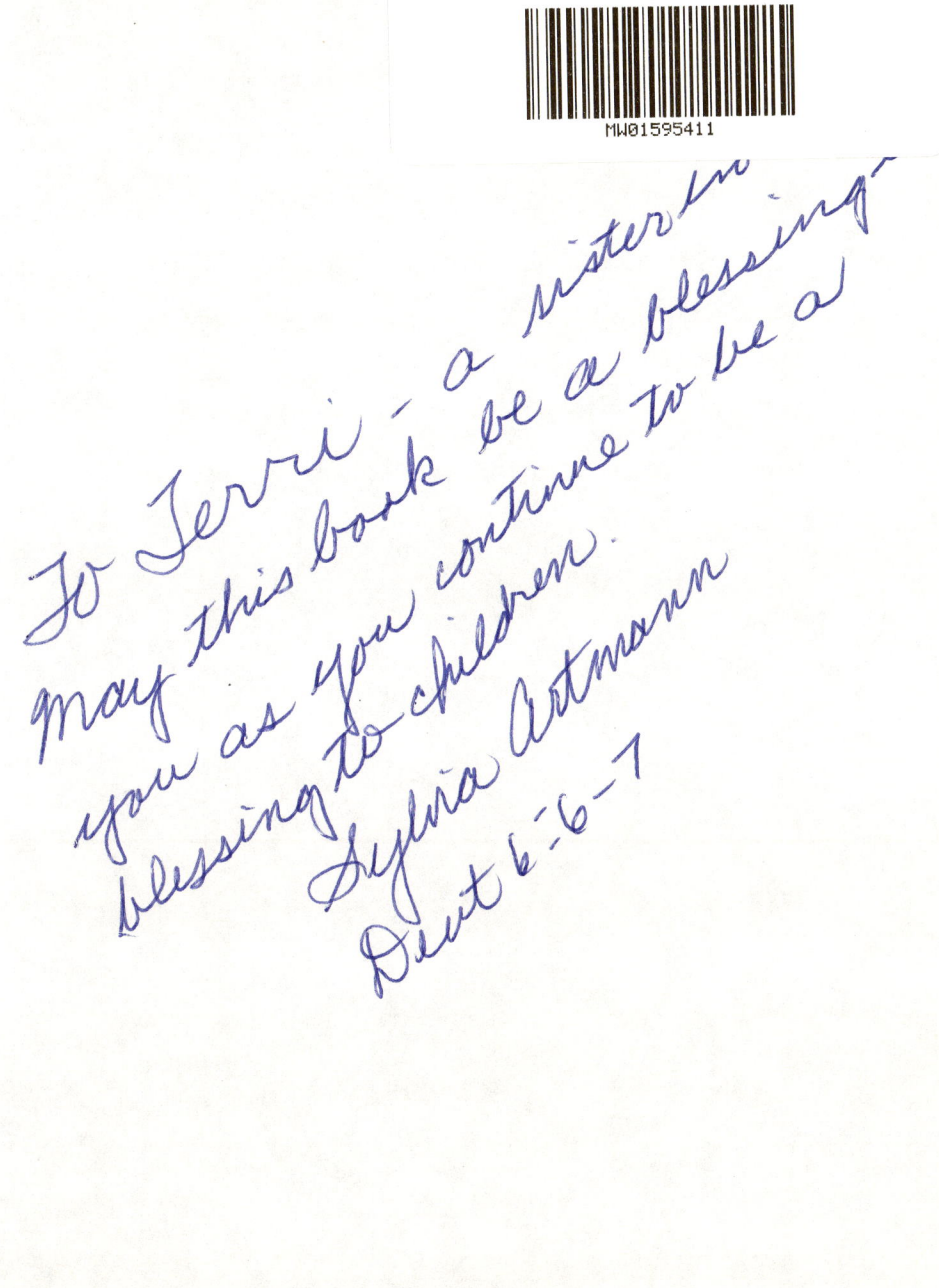

To Terri - a sister in
may this book be a blessing
you as you continue to be a
blessing to children.
Sylvia Artmann
Deut 6:6-7

Called To Teach

A GUIDEBOOK FOR THE JOURNEY

Sylvia Artmann

ISBN: 978-1-4624-0072-0 (sc)
ISBN: 978-1-4624-0071-3 (e)

Library of Congress Control Number: 2012932794

Inspiring Voices books may be ordered through booksellers or by contacting:

Inspiring Voices
1663 Liberty Drive
Bloomington, IN 47403
www.inspiringvoices.com
1-(866) 697-5313

Printed in the United States of America

Inspiring Voices rev. date: 3/13/2012

All quotations from the Bible are from the New King James Version.

CONTENTS

"I will instruct you and teach you in the way you should
go; I will guide you with My eye."Psalm 32:8

"And we know that all things work together for
good to those who love God, to those who are
called according to His purpose." Romans 8:28

CHAPTER 1

What Have I Got Myself Into ?!

"Not that we are sufficient of ourselves to think of anything as being from ourselves, but our sufficiency is from God." II Corinthians 3:5

The young woman shifted nervously from one foot to the other as she stood in the door of my office in the education division of a small Christian university. "I've always loved children," she said hesitantly. "I guess I should have majored in education to begin with. But I just didn't have all my goals in place when I first came to the university, and now I find myself with a degree that I really don't want to follow for my life's work. I think God is calling me to be a teacher, and I have an offer from a Christian school to teach. What can you do to help me? Is there a book I could read to help me to be prepared ?"

I fidgeted uneasily in my chair. She was not the first student to come to me with such a request. Certainly I did not think that one book could take the place of a complete course of study in teacher education, but there were many students who, because of having a university degree, were being invited to teach in Christian schools where pastors or educational directors had confidence in their character and dedication. Several had take one of my courses in educational methods and thus trusted me to help them. I had searched in vain for an effective book of this nature, since I feel that biblical precepts should be wedded with methods validated by educational research. Surely I have an obligation before God, I mused, to see that these dedicated young people are equipped to serve in this important role, for many would pursue the opportunity with or without further preparation. In addition, the Lord prompted me to realize that many parents are currently engaged in home schooling their own children. Perhaps they are not geographically close enough to attend a Christian school, or there are budget constraints, or perhaps they simply desire a closer bond and influence on their children's lives. Whatever the reason, few of these parents have ever had formal educational methods courses. They, too, needed the tools to do the very best job of teaching their children.

Christian education should be the very best that can be provided, whether at the preschool, grammar school, high school, or university level. This has always been a major precept of mine; and as a professor of education over the past twenty-eight years, I had felt obligated to defend this precept many times. When students had come to me complaining that my courses were "too hard; because, after all, isn't this a Christian school ?" I had felt it my responsibility to explain why my courses are consistently challenging. To me, Christian education should have even higher standards than the best of secular education. Scripture guides us in this by saying "Study to show thyself approved unto God; a workman that needeth not to be ashamed, rightly dividing the word of truth." II Timothy 2:15. It is not kind, either to the university students or to their future charges, to allow them to "slide by" with little challenge. True Christian love is demonstrated in helping others to be the best that they can be, taking full advantage of the talents that God has given to each one.

Nevertheless, I know that in many instances it is customary for Christian schools to hire any person of good moral character and intention who has a university degree of any sort. Christian character and morals are indeed important, but these fine young people need to be given the tools to teach, so that they will not be overcome with the demands natural to being an effective teacher. Similarly, many parents are extremely bright and able, in addition to being highly motivated to teach their children. Should such willing but untrained parents be abandoned to randomly experiment and succeed or fail as they struggle to provide the best education for their children? If so, this isn't far from the historical perspective when it was believed that any intelligent, literate person could teach. However, there has been so much research into how to facilitate the process, it seems a shame for dedicated Christian teachers not to have at least the rudiments of such information available to them. This is not to say that God cannot lead an untrained person to become a good teacher. I know this can happen. Yet, He has allowed me to learn much through study and personal experience in teaching over the past thirty-five years. Could it be that He was now calling me to share some of these truths with beginning or prospective teachers who have not had the opportunities for study that I have had?

It was a disturbing thought. As Professor of Education in this small, Christian university, I had a "number of bases to cover." I taught a full load of courses each semester, supervised student teachers, served as Certification Officer, and was Faculty Sponsor for the pre-professional Student Educators' Association. Additionally, of course, I had committee responsibilities, advisory responsibilities, and a number of students seeking me for counseling in their individual lives. When could I ever find time for such a major project? But, I know God never calls us to do what He does not provide the strength and wisdom to accomplish. For over five years I wrestled with this calling, constantly becoming more aware that it is, indeed, a calling. And so this book was born, and a new chapter in my life begins. Perhaps **you** are part of the reason that He called me to write this book. I pray that it can be of assistance to you.

CHAPTER II

Created In His Image:
In The Beginning

"For You formed my inward parts; You covered me in my mother's womb. I will praise You, for I am fearfully and wonderfully made. Marvelous are your works, and that my soul knows very well." Psalm 139:14

Do you expect me to put up with THAT ?

Many of the characteristics of young children try our patience until we feel we should teach them to respond and act more like "civilized" adults! But, have you ever stopped to think that God could have created children just like adults from the beginning if He had wanted to do so? Therefore, there must be a reason that they have short attention spans, don't really understand abstractions, learn primarily through firsthand use of their muscles and senses, etc. So, it seems that the effective teacher must seek to understand the child just the way God created him to be at various ages and stages, then use that information to more effectively teach. This doesn't mean that we should not try to "stretch" children in various ways to help them become more mature in behavior. But it does mean that we should learn what is reasonable to expect at various ages.

Why do we attempt to change children from the way God created them to be during developmentally different ages ? Well, in order to work with a group of children, it is indeed necessary to create an orderly, efficient (within limits), and relatively quiet environment.

Otherwise, the learning situation can quickly turn into chaos, where nothing of worth can be achieved. But, if we become intent on this orderly environment as being a higher priority than the needs of our students, we are forgetting that the main goal of the teacher should be to reach children and help them gain academically, physically, morally, spiritually, and emotionally. This will only occur if school is "a good place to be" from the student's perspective. Think about it for yourself. Did you embrace learning and show changes of behavior for the better when you encountered a teacher who made you feel foolish, inadequate, or uncomfortable ? Of course not. So, let's look at how we can balance the need to avoid classroom chaos with respect for the child's developmental needs and capabilities.

How can I make children WANT to behave and learn?

Unfortunately, you **can't** make them. The answer lies in **motivating** them. You've heard the old adage, "You can lead a horse to water, but you can't make him drink!" It's the same way with children. However, what can we do to help that horse **want** to drink? We can feed him salt! Similarly, there are certain ways of working with children that will "woo" them into wanting to do what they should do. First of all, knowledge of expected developmental characteristics of children at various ages and stages is power. It helps teachers to "go with the flow" but also provide gentle, appropriate "shaping." An ideal role model of this is provided by God as our Divine Teacher. "But God demonstrates His own love toward us in that while we were yet sinners, Christ died for us." (Romans 5:8) God loved us just the way we were. We didn't have to earn it by good behavior. He recognized our weaknesses even better than we could. Scripture tells us, "For He knows our frame; He remembers that we are dust." (Psalm 103:14) Nevertheless, although He loved us just the way we were, He also loved us too much to leave us that way. He said, "Be ye therefore holy, as I am holy." (I Peter 1:16) Life in His kingdom is a constant process of being "wooed" by His love and constant support to become all that we are capable of being. Similarly, the loving, encouraging teacher draws children upward and onward into maturity in every area. As we place the children's needs above our own (and primary among their needs is self control, so this does not mean allowing chaos), we will be following the lead of Christ. He left His throne in Glory because He and His Father saw our need. So, we must love the children too much to leave them just as they are. It is in their own best interest that they grow, both academically and behaviorally.

By understanding and responding to our students' developmental characteristics and demonstrating loving behavior even when it interferes with meeting our own needs, we are showing respect for them as fellow beings uniquely created by God. But it is imperative that they be held to the standard of respecting us as teachers, as well. On the checklist I used in evaluating student teachers as they conducted a lesson, there is an area to be rated called "Creates a respectful classroom." Many times I had to give a student teacher a lower mark in this area while noting, "Although you are definitely respectful and encouraging to your students, you are allowing them to show disrespect for yourself by a) not listening when you are giving instructions, b) not obeying the classroom rules, or c) refusing to follow instructions." (Other misbehaviors also demonstrate disrespect, but these are the most common.) There will always be children who will do these things to "see what you will do about it" in class. Therefore, my student teachers only received a lowered rating when they allowed such behavior to continue. As I said, much of the time such behavior is a test to see what the teacher or parent will do. So, plan in advance what your response should be. Be assured that all the children present will be noting how you respond, so (either for good or for bad) your behavior will be showing respectful (or disrespectful) expectations to more than just the one child involved.

First of all, always make the correction in a firm, but quiet and controlled manner. Remember, "The wrath of man does not produce the righteousness of God." (James 1:20) To the child who is talking or not paying attention while you are giving instructions, you could say something like, "Johnny, it is important that you listen to this so that you will know how to complete your project correctly (or learn important things about plants, etc.). When it is your time to share, I promise I will listen and not talk while you are talking. I expect you to show me that same respect."

You may be surprised at their response. They already know, or need to learn if they do not, what is meant by the word "respect." As a matter of fact, that's a good character trait worthy of devoting a complete lesson to teaching. If there is not enough time for a complete lesson, brainstorm with the children what the word means; especially at a time when you use the word in a situation like this. If a child has caused a disturbance and all eyes are on you to see how you will handle it, this creates the much lauded "teachable moment" to have a short lesson on the meaning of "respect" and why it is important. Even if you have to take ten minutes away from teaching math, reading, or social studies; this may be, by far, the most important thing you teach all day! Good teachers always have a plan for how they will use their time during classes (Otherwise, time slips away and is wasted. If you aim at nothing, you hit it every time!). However, the truly effective teacher is aware that such "teachable moments" yield more vivid, and thus more fully remembered, learning as compared with standard plans. And frequently the learning is of a moral/spiritual nature, which is majorly important, but difficult to teach without a real life situation as an example. Thus, the truly excellent teacher is well-planned, but flexible!

If the cause for discussing possible disrespect is a lack of following the classroom rules, you might say something like this, "Johnny, I'm afraid you are forgetting the rule we have at school about _____. Can you tell me what that rule is and why it is important?" Of course, in order to do this you will have to make the rules plain at the beginning of school and be consistent about reinforcing obedience to those rules. Although as an authority under God it may be tempting to say, "You do this because I say so!" it is important for the children to understand that you, as a loving authority figure, have instituted this rule for their own good. So, there's every reason to help them see why the rule is there. (ex. "If everyone is talking at once, we can't hear the instructions. So, we have a rule that only one person talks at a time during large group time. Also. Such behavior violates the rule that we will show respect for each other at all times.") If you can't think of a good reason (for the children's benefit) that you have a rule, perhaps you should reconsider whether or not to have it! However, after you are convinced that it is a needed rule and have explained those reasons to the class, if some of the children still want to say, "That's not fair," (etc.,etc.), then you have another responsibility. Say to the class, "I'm sorry some of you do not agree with my rule, but as the adult and teacher, it is my responsibility under God to provide the best environment for each child in my classroom. Because I love you and know that you are not always mature enough to know what is best for you, I must have obedience to the rule."

Another reason given for a student possibly showing disrespect calls for a firmer hand because it includes the phrase "refusing to." When a child refuses to do what he/she knows should be done, it is a definite example of willfulness. This is the kind of disobedience James Dobson mentions as being totally unacceptable (and I wholly agree). First of all, when confronting a defiant child, do not do so from across the room. If you are working with another student or a group of students, first excuse yourself to them for leaving unexpectedly (they'll understand, but respect you more for showing that courtesy to them), and walk across the room to the child in question. Get down on his/her level, place your hand gently but firmly on the child's shoulder, look into his eyes and say, "I'm sorry, but if you continue to _____, you are choosing to _____ (whatever is your previously announced type of discipline consequences--see Chapter XIII)" By using the words "You are choosing to," you are letting the child know he still has a chance to behave correctly and escape punishment. This, however, should be the **only** warning. If the child continues in the defiant behavior, it is the responsibility of the teacher to see that consequences immediately follow. Many classroom discipline plans fail because teachers are always giving "three chances," or eternally "one more chance," etc. They think they do this out of love for the child, but it is in the child's best interest to have **one** warning (being sure he/she understands the rule and its consequences) and then having to "pay the price," (which, by the way, should not be too painful. It is said that beginning teachers have a tendency to "use cannons to kill little sparrows.")

If the consequence is a natural consequence to the rule broken, it will cause better learning. For instance, the child who is repeatedly not respecting the rights of others in the play group may be asked to sit out of play for a measured amount of time. Actually, one minute per year of the child's age is frequently enough for demonstrating the need for correction, yet showing the teacher is truly "on his side" and has a desire to reinstate him for "another chance." Five-year-olds required to sit on the sidelines for five minutes will sit and squirm the entire time in most instances (watch them). At the end of that time, call the child to yourself, ask why he had to "sit out," and what will be different now. Send the forgiven offender back to play with a "Go and sin no more" attitude. Remember--Christ is our role model! We couldn't do it on our own. Human nature is too easily irritated!.

Teachers sometimes ban children from the playground for the entire play period, or from recess for a week. Such punishments are excessive and lead to resentment and additional "sneaky" unacceptable and increasingly rebellious behavior. When it is necessary to call a child down for additional examples of the undesirable behavior, the length of time-out may need to be increased (moderately), but it is also important that the teacher demonstrate sadness, not anger, at the offense. Instead of, "Well, you haven't learned your lesson, have you?" or an "Aha ! I caught you!" attitude, the teacher needs to demonstrate disappointment and sadness, mete out appropriate punishment, and then restore the child for another chance, telling him, "This time, I just know you'll remember, so we won't have to do this again!" Remember, our most effective discipline occurs with children when we demonstrate that we are on their side, helping them to remember to be better for their own sake, not just punishing them because they are annoying to us and we are angry. Search your own heart to be sure that this is true. I f the child's behavior has "gotten to you" and you really feel only anger toward him, take it to the Lord and ask Him for wisdom.

The keynote philosophy on which effective classroom management should be built, then, is encompassed by the demonstration and reinforcement of mutual respect between teacher and student. This must flow in both directions; and when not the case, corrections should be made as firmly and kindly as possible. If not, classroom management will be like the "house built upon the sand" described by Christ in His parable in Matthew 7. When the rains descended and the floods came, the house fell, and great was the fall of it. Mutual respect is the foundation on the rock described in that parable. When tough times come in a classroom that is based on mutual respect, that firm foundation will enable teachers and students to restore peace and order. Many "techniques" are effective in establishing and maintaining such order, but this foundation stone is the most important of all. We'll discuss these techniques in the chapter about classroom management.

In order to treat children fairly, with both the respect and firmness that they need, it is almost essential that the teacher, at least for the most part, enjoy children and teaching. There is an old saying, for which I have been unable to find the source, that says, "Perhaps there is no responsibility as underrated as the responsibility for being happy." What?! How can anyone give you a **responsibility** for being happy? Can you just turn emotions on and off like this ? No, but as many psychologists can tell you, emotions follow behavior. If you behave according to the emotions you would like to be feeling, the emotions will usually follow. If you want to love someone, figure out what you would do for that person if you loved him, and then do it ! Amazingly enough, that advice is given by many marriage counselors, and if given time it works.

Therefore, figure out, "If I were really enjoying children the way God made them (active, inquisitive, enthusiastic, playful), how would I act ?" Well, first of all you'd probably "lighten up" a little, see that it's OK to have fun with children, and provide an appropriate place for legitimate child behaviors (such as making noise and running) to occur within the schedule. As you find yourself switching from "How can I get through this school day?" to "Let's find out exciting things about God's world together," you may just find the children responding differently to you than before. And, in turn, you hopefully will decide that although teaching is hard work, it is also richly rewarding. Why is it so important that you **enjoy** children and teaching ? You probably have heard the old saying, "When Mama ain't (sic) happy, ain't nobody happy." Well, in like manner to the mother of a home, the teacher greatly prescribes the emotional tone of her classroom.

Finally, and perhaps of most importance, pray that God will give you His love for these children and His wisdom in dealing with them. Such a prayer, sincerely uttered, will bring about a miraculous change in your perspective. I have been teaching at various levels and in various capacities for over 30 years, and occasionally I'll find a student who really "gets under my skin." On the occasions when I have been wise, I have prayed and said, "Lord, I know you made this student and you love him, but I just can't seem to do it. Please help me to feel Your love for him flowing through me." When I have been faithful to pray this, I have been amazed at how the Lord has opened my eyes to see sterling qualities about this person that I had never seen before ! It's almost eerie to see a student you previously could hardly tolerate become a favorite of yours! (Why is it we pray about something and then are amazed to see God grant it ?!)

So, relax and enjoy the wonderful, God-given qualities of young children, like enthusiasm, curiosity, and spontaneity; while gradually motivating them to mature out of characteristics like selfishness, disorganization, and lack of self control. Sounds clear-cut, doesn't it? But it's far from easy. I myself keep having to say, "Teach me again, Lord. I forget." Life is a journey. We don't reach any worthwhile destination overnight. Teaching also is a process of developing and improving. Don't be too hard on yourself if you aren't perfect yet-- none of us will be until we get to Heaven! As a matter of fact, if you get to the point that you think you have everything "all together," you probably have a serious problem! After over 30 years of teaching, I'm constantly learning ways I need to grow and improve. And that's the way it should be.

CHAPTER III

The Early Years:
Our Greatest Opportunity

**"Then they also brought infants to Him that He might
touch them, but when the disciples saw it, they rebuked
them. But Jesus called them to Him and said, 'Let the
little children come unto me, and do not forbid them;
for of such is the kingdom of God.'" Luke 18: 15-16**

Much secular research is currently being conducted concerning brain
development. The more we learn about it, the more scientists are
convinced that the very earliest years are our greatest opportunity to
help a child reach his intellectual potential. Experiments have even
been done to prove that learning is occurring in the womb! While it is
frightening to think that overly-conscientious parents may be literally
"piping Sesame Street into the womb," nevertheless this research is
dispelling the harmful previous image of the preschool child as being
too young to actually learn.

As long as we do not violate the basic nature of how God planned
for learning to occur in the early years, we should realize that young
children are capable of learning far more than had previously been
suspected. Preschool teachers should now have the respect of the
educational world as being "more than baby sitters." As a matter of
fact, many secular educators are now offering evidence that money
spent on educating children carefully during preschool years may be
more important than money spent in the upper grades trying to re-

claim those children who did not have helpful early education. The Perry Preschool Project has followed results in children that attended quality preschools and compared them with children from similar backgrounds at the age of 27, finding tremendous results. They have calculated that one dollar spent in appropriate education of preschool children from disadvantaged areas saves society seven dollars in results over those intervening years. This results from such children being gainfully-employed tax payers, rather than drawing money on the welfare roles. Well, you may say, "My child isn't disadvantaged." Or, "I don't teach in a disadvantaged area." Even if that is true, should good results not also translate into gains for the children we teach ? And, we must also remember our Lord's admonishment to "be our brother's keeper."

With these things in mind, let's take a look at how the young child (from age three to six years) typically learns in the most effective way. Although those early days and months following birth are very important, since most of you as Christian school teachers will be dealing with children after they reach age three, we'll start there.

Leaving infancy behind: the three year old

Three-year-olds are typically leaving the "baby stage," yet often regress to babyish ways when tired, ill, or frustrated in any way. Although they are eager to "do things with the big boys," they are easily tired by their efforts to keep up, and may therefore become teary-eyed, suck their thumbs, or withdraw into a depressed or anxious state. It is a primary responsibility with three-year-olds to encourage them to try new things, yet provide much opportunity for rest and replenishment of blood sugar through nutritious snacks. They are usually eager to please adults rather than being rebellious, yet prone to be "clingy" if in new situations.

Years ago, there was a classic set of child development films on the "ages and stages" of children. These films contained much truth about the nature of children at various ages. However, experience and research have since taught us that the techniques recommended by the films were far too permissive. In other words, children's basic developmental nature at various ages has not changed, but even secular psychology's preferred methods of dealing with that nature have changed. The first film in that series was entitled "The Terrible Twos and the Trusting Threes." The next film was "The Frustrating Fours and the Fascinating Fives." One basic truth that the films sought to impart was the fact that children go through stages of feeling confident and outgoing (sometimes to the extreme of being rebellious about outside control), followed by periods of compliance and dependence (sometimes to the extreme of being whiny and clingy). Thus, at two years of age, many psychologists have characterized the stage as being represented by a "No, I won't" mentality; thus named the "terrible twos." The threes, on the other hand, have been characterized as "trusting," because they are more docile and willing to follow parental suggestions or commands. Similarly, fours are "frustrating" as they seek their own way independently, and fives are "fascinating" because they desire to learn from and please adults.

Not all children hit these stages at exactly the same age. The "terrible two" assertiveness may occur at eighteen months or not until thirty months, for example. Other stages are also approximate in age. However, time and research have borne out that, indeed, children do alternate between periods of independence and dependence as they move through the early childhood years. Which periods are easiest on the parents and teachers, however, will vary with the child's basic personality. For example, my oldest daughter seemed to be fiercely independent from birth. She was one of the children James Dobson describes in his book *The Difficult Child* as "coming into the world smoking a cigar and ordering the delivery room nurses around." For us as parents and for her, the twos and fours were very difficult stages. We were relieved at ages three and five, thinking (in our own naive way as first-time parents), that the tough times were over and we finally had learned how to "parent" wisely. But, for such children it seems that every stage forms a more difficult bump in the road than it does for other children. I praise God that He has brought her through many difficult experiences to emerge as a dedicated Christian, a successful MD. and a loving, compassionate wife, mother, and daughter to us. This is all to say that most of the time "difficult" children have much to offer the world, and are worth any extra effort it takes to "bring them through." They will certainly keep you on your knees, as parents and teachers should be, anyway!

Our second daughter was very different from her older sister. She was very quiet, compliant, and eager to please. These seemed to be wonderful traits, but they caused a reverse response to the "ages and stages" described. One stage described by developmental psychiatrists to arise around eight to twelve months of age is "stranger anxiety," when babies sometimes refuse to have anyone but their closest care giver (usually their mother) take care of them. They are terrified of anyone else, and in an unfamiliar situation sometimes will not even allow that closest person out of their sight without screaming. With my oldest child, I did not believe in the existence of such a stage. She loved everybody and would smile and go to anyone who wanted to hold her. My second daughter demonstrated all the terror described above when we went to my husband's hometown when she was nine months old. She would not let me out of her sight! Accordingly, the "terrible twos" formed a good time for her--she demonstrated more independence and willingness to try new things on her own. The "trusting threes," however, were characterized by much whining and clinging.

So, the main thing to remember is that periods of dependence and independence tend to alternate as children grow and develop, and according to the basic temperament of the child, some periods will be easier on parents and teachers than others. The important concept here is that, in all stages we are loving the child and accepting him, yet lovingly providing guidance and reassurance so that he will not become too rebellious or too terrified and therefore become "stuck" in the undesirable stage because his needs have not been met. With proper understanding, support, patience, and much prayer, the child will move into a more desirable stage before long. But never think your challenges as a teacher or parent are over!

The four-year-old: on the go and out of bounds!

Four-year-olds are generally "out to conquer the world!" They are feeling much more confident than at three, and their own overconfidence can get them into big trouble, since they are still greatly lacking in maturity! This is the time to go over safety precautions about the use of outdoor playground equipment or other accident-prone situations, explaining the reasons. It's a good mental exercise to ask them to tell you the safety rules before going into such an area. It will sharpen their recall skills (so important for success in school and in life!) as well as keep safety consciousness uppermost in their minds. Nevertheless, teachers should remain in close supervision at all times. Sometimes we credit the four-year-old with more maturity than he possesses, based on his advanced speech and amazing reasoning powers.

Four-year-olds are also frequently characterized by "out of bounds" behavior. They must constantly be reminded, gently but firmly, of the rules and the reasons for those rules. This may be the stage when they openly defy you and the rules of the classroom, as their language development can allow them to be quite "sassy." It is important that you, as the teacher, remain calm in the face of what may even include some "bathroom language" they have picked up from wrong TV shows, or even from their parents at home. They need to be told that such words and behavior are not allowed at school. (Be careful about saying, "Nice people don't talk like that," since their parents may speak that way.)

Ready to cooperate (sometimes): the five-year-old

Five-year-olds have usually reached a delightful stage. As a matter of fact, when their children arrive at this stage parents frequently begin to congratulate themselves for having used whatever parenting method they have chosen, as five-year-olds are more prone to cooperate with adults than at any previous stage. Even the physical appearance of the child indicates that he is rapidly moving out of the chubby, impulsive toddler look into the appearance of the young adult he is destined to become. Around the world, even in cultures that do not mark children's ages as we do, adults begin to expect more out of children as they move into this period. This is known in psychological circles as the "five-to-seven shift." As children slim down and lose their first baby teeth during this period, their appearance seems to announce to the world that they are ready for increased learning and responsibilities. However, they are still characterized by a need to learn in much the same way that younger children do (especially up until around seven), so first let's look in the next chapter at some of those recommended techniques for children from three- to six- years old.

CHAPTER IV

Combining Young Children With Curriculum: An Awesome Responsibility

"But whoever causes one of these little ones who believe in Me to stumble, it would be better for him if a millstone were hung around his neck, and he were thrown into the sea." Mark 9:42

Wow, are they active!

As you watch a group of three-to-five-year-old children interacting in a play yard, most people are impressed by how busy and on-the-go they are. They would rather run than walk, and they are excited about doing everything in an active, rather than a passive, way. This gives us a good cue about how they would learn most effectively, for as we observe how God has created these children we receive insight on dealing with them. Children have been learning actively through exploring the wonders of their world every moment of their lives until they come to school.. Unfortunately, sometimes when they get to school their learning stops, or at least diminishes. They are taught to sit quietly and wait (which can be a good thing if not overdone), and they are "talked at" instead of "worked with." Although children under seven definitely <u>can</u> learn by listening, this is not their primary learning modality. The younger they are, the more they need to learn through actually touching, manipulating, and exploring the concepts we seek to teach them. They are not primarily "pencil and paper" oriented yet. Although they may need to have a worksheet to record on paper something they have learned previously in a more active manner, too often they are told to sit quietly and work with pencil and paper for the largest portion of the school day.

Children can best learn to write the alphabet first through following sandpaper letters with their finger, tracing letters in the sand, modeling them with clay, etc. They can learn to recognize letters and sounds by matching letter cards that are alike, playing letter bingo, or having a "letter week" in which they bring objects from home that begin with that letter, drawing the letter in shaving cream on the tables (makes the whole classroom smell good, too!), and/or cooking a food that begins with that letter. All of these ways of learning are more exciting and vivid than just using worksheets, and psychologists have proven through research that children retain what they have learned more effectively if that learning is vivid. Similarly, math concepts can be learned through manipulatives such as puzzles that have a numeral on one side needing to be joined together with the proper number of objects on the other side. Shapes can be learned by cutting out cookies in various shapes to bake. After the simplest numerical concepts have been learned, children can write addition or subtraction equations as a result of using counters such as small plastic bears, or, in the absence of the budget to purchase these, parents can help you save the plastic tops off gallon milk jugs to use as counters.

Children's large muscles mature before their small muscles. This means that the child who has great difficulty in cutting with scissors and writing his letters would benefit from additional time in assembling puzzles, working with modeling clay, and stringing large beads to match a pictured pattern. Many concepts can be taught in a large-muscle manner to a child who is experiencing frustration with the fine-motor skills. One of the biggest challenges for a teacher is the fact that whenever you get as many as five students of the same age together, there will be some who find a developmentally-average task too easy and thus may be bored, while others will find it too difficult and become frustrated. A good teacher's task, then, is to individualize instruction. (Nobody ever promised you that teaching would be easy!)

Individualization occurs through first observing the children in your class. A major part of every teacher's job is to observe and see what is working, and with which children. We need for children to be challenged, but not frustrated. So as we allow them to experience various concepts by experiencing the way the teacher has set up her classroom, we diagnose and prescribe for future lessons. Our goal may be to have all children learn to form their names legibly in manuscript. Yet our method may need to vary considerably. One child may already be printing, so we want to help him/her print on lined paper. Another child may need to trace over his name with his finger many times or form the letters in clay over a card on which the teacher has printed his name in large letters with black marker. Certain letters are harder than others to form correctly, and children often have difficulty with reversing their letters, particularly the letter "S." In these cases especially it is good to allow plenty of time to trace and manipulate before becoming concerned that the child has a learning disability. Too often, such "labels" result in the parents (and ultimately the child) believing that there is a problem (whether or not one actually exists) and creating a "self-fulfilling prophecy." Reversals are quite common, and due to the level of the brain development (which causes mirror images from one hemisphere of the brain to the other during this period), reversals of letters or numerals should not be a cause for concern until around seven years of age.

But shouldn't they be able to sit and listen in a large group ?

Young children learn much more effectively one-on-one with an adult or individually interacting with materials than they do in large groups. It has been said that a young child only has an attention span of approximately the number of minutes that is the same as his years of age. Actually I think, through personal experience in teaching, that this is incorrect and varies a great deal with the child. It also varies with the type of activity. When a child makes a natural choice to engage in exploration or interaction with sensory materials, even the very young may exhibit attention spans five or six times as many minutes as their ages would indicate. The key here is that the child is naturally motivated, thus he will become absorbed and not be distracted.

The problem arises when the teacher tries to work with a large group of children at a time. Although some may remain motivated and attentive, there are almost always those who do not. Some will sit quietly without disturbing, but will not be learning anything (too often we are not even aware that these children have "spaced out"). Others (to our distress) will be bothering everyone around them. We do want to gradually "stretch" children's ability to sit attentively in a large group, but the best way to do this is to start with short periods of large group experiences, gradually adding more time. And the key to doing this is in a role that is highly important for any teacher, but especially so for an early childhood teacher-- **observing**. A wise teacher will learn to constantly scan her group for 1) signs of unrest, 2) lack of eye contact, and 3) low response to questioning. These cues will indicate when it is time to "move on" to small group, center, and/or individual activities.

But don't you sometimes have to use large group instruction?

Preschool children do need, however, to be gently encouraged to attend to instruction delivered in a large group setting. Otherwise, they will not be successful as they get into higher grades in school. The secret lies in **challenging but not frustrating**; a concept that transfers into every area of teaching children, whether cognitively, socially, emotionally, or even spiritually. For those times when large group work is conducted, it is important to make it as interesting as possible in order to hold the children's natural interest. A preschool teacher needs to be rather dramatic in the way she shares group information or reads a story to a large group. Stopping to make intermittent comments and asking questions of various children will also help to keep their minds engaged. Giving them something to "listen for" in the story, and a concrete response to make when they hear it, will also help extend their interest.

For example, before you begin reading the story, always relate the children's lives to what you are going to read. Perhaps you might say,

"Have you ever felt that you wanted to play with other children, but you didn't know how to get started ? Listen to this story about a little rabbit who had that problem. When you hear something that he decided to do that was a good idea, give me a 'thumbs up.' When you hear something he decided to do that wasn't a good idea, give me a 'thumbs down.'" (Of course, you would have previously established with the class how to give a "thumbs up" and "thumbs down" response, and what these responses mean.)

This technique, by the way, is a good way to test for group involvement. It is known as EPRT (Every Pupil Response Technique) because it requires all children to indicate they are "with you" and ready to respond. It also is a quick way to test informally whether children have understood something taught to them previously. Make a statement of something you have previously taught them and say, "If you agree with this statement, give me a 'thumbs up.' If you disagree, give me a 'thumbs down.' If you aren't sure, turn your thumbs to the side." This is actually a valuable tool, even in the upper grades, as a quick index of whether or not something needs to be retaught.

In addition to the fact that young children have relatively short attention spans, they also have difficulty in sitting still for long periods of time. They are growing physically so rapidly that their muscles may actually begin to ache if they are not given periodic chances to stretch them. It is a wise teacher who plans for the children to have alternating times of physical activity and quiet learning activity. The key is to keep each period short, so as to avoid the aching muscles and lack or attention, but also avoiding the tendency for children to get too "wild" if they have a long period of an exciting game or other intense physical activity. Again, by the all-important role of **observing**, the teacher will develop an intuition concerning each individual group for when they are losing interest and when they are becoming too "wound up."

How can I really reach young children in the way they learn best ?

There is an old Chinese proverb that says, "I hear and I forget; I see and I remember; I do and I understand." This is a good thing to remember in teaching any age of student. However, with the young child it is an absolute necessity to remember. Experiencing a concept, rather than just hearing about it, is the way God prepared children to make sense out of their world. And it's really more exciting for both the child and the teacher when learning takes place in that manner, anyway!

The younger the child, the greater the need to involve as many of the five senses as possible in order to facilitate his learning. If the child can hear it, see it, touch it, and possibly even smell and taste it, he is more likely to retain it ! That's one reason cooking with children is such an effective way of teaching all the different parts of the curriculum. We'll talk more about that later.

One great, God-given advantage that young children have (which diminishes with age) is an ability to hear and replicate language sounds. An infant is born with the ability to make all language sounds; but as he listens to the language around him, he systematically drops those sounds he does not hear. He then babbles only with the sounds of the surrounding language. Thus "practice" with language begins in infancy. Linguists can listen to an audio tape of an infant babbling during the second half of the first year and tell you whether that infant is from an English-speaking culture, a Chinese-speaking culture, or any other culture the linguist has studied extensively.

Similarly, from around 18 months to 36 months, linguists feel that children are "linguistic geniuses," being able to master two and three languages simultaneously if they are spoken by different caregivers during this time. They do not confuse the languages or use them with the wrong care giver, either! God has truly prepared children as they come into the world to master this most important area-- communication! There is a sensitivity to language which will never occur again. It is said that if a child learns a language before age five, there will be no "accent " to show that this was not the language of his primary culture. This is because he so clearly hears the sounds in all their complexity and has the ability to replicate them.

Preschool children are thus fascinated by language sounds. Piaget, a highly respected educational theorist, gave the name "functional assimilation" to the tendency of a child to want to practice those things that he is naturally and developmentally learning . It's a natural process that good teachers should capitalize upon. You've probably noticed how young children love rhymes and rhythm (witness the popularity of Mother Goose through the ages). They also like to "play with" nonsensical sounds. (Dr. Seuss certainly took advantage of that in making his books so popular with young children!) Teachers can also take advantage of this developmental sensitivity to sounds.

Instead of the multitude of worksheets seen in many preschools, teachers need to capitalize on language games that emphasize rhyming and natural phonics. A good preparation for reading is to read aloud to the children from a book that rhymes, stopping right before the rhyming word and allowing the children to chorus a word that rhymes and "makes sense." This utilizes both forms of reading instruction-- skills (phonics) and holistic instruction (meaning).

Various unit themes or seasonal themes can be used for games related to specific beginning sounds, as well. For example, a tree could be outlined on butcher paper attached to the bulletin board in the fall and die-cut leaves provided in different fall colors. The teacher could then talk about leaves, emphasizing the way the word "leaves" begins, and having the children tell words beginning with the "l" sound to place upon the tree. These could be lettered in broad tip marker and put on the tree, so the more advanced children could take a pointer and "read the room" during free choice time.

Do not underestimate children's natural ability, through sound sensitivity, to solve linguistic challenges. They love to "put on their thinking caps" and solve a riddle such as "Who do you suppose this person is ? Her name starts with 'M' and rhymes with 'brother.' " As a matter of fact, sometimes when their attention in large group is wandering (good for you--you saw it beginning to happen!), the statement of "riddle-a-diddle, riddle-a-diddle! I have a riddle for you!" will get them back, at least for a short time.

Additionally, it is important to help children to recognize visual likenesses and differences in preparation for seeing, for example, the difference between a "b" and a "d." However, these visual comparisons can be taught through sight Bingo or matching cards, puzzle pieces, etc. instead of one tiresome worksheet after another. And since the visual sense is not as highly developed in the young child as the sound sensitivity, it seems appropriate to capitalize first upon their natural ability to excel in sound recognition.

This sensitivity to sounds includes a natural response to tone, pitch, and rate of the teacher's (or other adult's) voice. Knowledge of this is very important to classroom management and prevention of discipline problems. When a problem occurs, the natural tendency (without being aware of it) is for the teacher to become agitated and talk more rapidly, loudly, and in a higher pitched voice. This, in turn, agitates the children further; and they become louder and more unruly. I have taught my student teachers to consciously slow down their voices and keep their pitch low and even when a problem occurs, speak quietly but firmly. They are amazed at how well this works (but also at how difficult it really is when the situation causes them to feel agitated!).

Is it good to get them excited, or can that be a problem ?

Like everything else, excitement in learning, although good, needs to be tempered with moderation. As adults, we are more prone to stick with a learning task if it is motivating and exciting. But young children have a tendency to become overly excited and even "hyper" if excitement leads to over-stimulation. It's part of the way God made them at this stage of development. Therefore, new and exciting activities need to be kept in moderation, worked into the expected daily routine, and announced to the children in advance.

This is a concept that I learned the hard way ! Having previously taught at the junior high level, when I took additional training to prepare myself for preschool teaching nobody had told me that the old saying, "variety is the spice of life," had to be interpreted cautiously at this younger age. I would have a wonderful "surprise" for the children (such as a special art activity that took longer than usual, a special guest, or a cooking activity that would take up a generous part of the morning). Instead of showing excitement and joy as the time went by, I realized that the children became agitated and seemed troubled. Some would even say, "Mrs. Artmann, we forgot calendar !" (or whatever else was being left out of our daily routine). Even though I would reassure them that it was fine, and that we were having a "special" morning today, they still went about with worried looks.

What I later learned from additional reading in the field of child development, was the fact that young children, perhaps because of their smaller size than the adults in their world, tend to feel rather powerless (unless they have been so overly indulged that they feel they are the "center of the universe!"). Upon reflection, I remembered how I had felt when I was quite small and forced to the back of an elevator with an adult lady's coat right up against my nose. Nobody had meant to be unkind, but I felt very small and powerless. Psychologists tell us that the feeling of powerlessness is the most uncomfortable of feelings, even for adults. Young children compensate somewhat for this powerless feeling by being able to predict "what comes next" in their routine. I had unwittingly taken this power away from my class by planning to "surprise" them ! A routine gives security to the children because they can predict what is coming next and mentally prepare for it.

This doesn't mean that a good early-childhood teacher never varies from the set routine. It simply means that it is very important to establish a schedule for activities and stick with it most of the time. When something new and exciting is going to happen, it is a good idea to talk about the change with the children for a couple of days in advance. Then, right before the children go home on the day before the change is to take place, ask, "Who can tell me what is going to be different tomorrow ?" They then can enter into the special activity with real enthusiasm. As a matter of fact, when there is something particularly exciting (like a field trip to the zoo), this creates a natural way to count the calendar days remaining before the upcoming event, discuss the day of the week it will occur, etc.

How much should preschool children be challenged to learn ?

As previously mentioned, we constantly strive to be **challenging but not frustrating.** An important part of this concept is worked out in presenting children with enough new information to interest them, yet with enough previously-learned information to help that former information to become permanent and to give the child a frame of reference within which to place the new information. A historically renowned educator by the name of J. McVicker Hunt said that the secret of all learning lay in what he called the **problem of the match.** His definition of the term was to make the amount of new information difficult enough to challenge, yet familiar enough to avoid frustration for the particular stage of the learner. As an example of the above concept in your own life, think about the content of this book. If you already know everything that is written here, you've probably already put the book down before getting this far, as you consider it to be boring. On the other hand, if you have no background knowledge about children or how they learn at all, you probably are beginning to think, "Why did I ever think I could do this ?"

Even if the teacher totally understands the above concept, implementing it in the classroom is far from simple ! Not all children respond to the same level of difficulty, even though they may be the same age or even the same developmentally. Some have a richer background of experiences and thus already know more than others. In addition, some have experienced a great deal of success in what they have done and therefore can "playfully entertain" possible answers to various questions or situations without becoming frustrated. Others, who may have already begun to consider themselves as "dumb" (sadly, some preschoolers have indeed adopted that label for themselves), learn much more effectively when most of the information is something they already know and feel confident about. This enables them to begin to see themselves as "smart."

In addition, repetition makes learning more permanent. It has been estimated that the average person needs to encounter a relatively simple new learning about twenty times before it becomes permanent, and some people or situations may require up to two hundred repetitions to become permanent ! So, intersperse the new with the familiar constantly in teaching. Even more effective is to show a student how a new learning fits into the framework he already knows. These "connections" will cause brain development and synaptic connections as well as help children to see that new information will be useful to them.

Isn't our goal for children more than just knowledge ?

Scripture wisely tells us that, "The fear of the Lord is the beginning of wisdom." Psalm 111:10 We don't just want our children to gain knowledge, but to "develop a heart of wisdom." The preschool is a prime time for moral development. Scholars differ on the exact time of the development of the conscience, but most agree that it is firmly in place (or sadly may not ever be in place) by the age of six years. Newer research is showing that children as young as eighteen months begin to demonstrate feelings of conscience. So, during the preschool years, dealings with moral development are vitally important.

There seem to be, according to moral development experts, three ways of looking at moral development: right thinking (cognitive), right actions/habits (behavioral), and right feelings (emotional). Since young children do not reason entirely as adults do, preschoolers seem to respond better to behavioral and emotional training in moral development.

The development of conscience, for instance, is an emotional feeling of guilt when a person does something he knows is wrong. Previously, psychologists have said that guilt was damaging and needed to be avoided at all costs. But, all truth being God's truth, scientists have observed what happens when there is no sense of guilt over anything. Such individuals develop into what is known as sociopaths: individuals who could murder their own parents in cold blood with no feelings of guilt. Nobody wants that for children--not even the most militant secularists! So, psychologists now realize that although too much guilt (and especially false guilt) can be damaging, a measured amount of guilt is necessary for good moral judgment.

If emotions are the key, how do we develop the right kinds of emotions?

Children tend to develop guilt over behaviors that emotionally distress an adult with whom they have formed a warm, loving bond. So the first step, both as parents and as teachers, is to develop that loving bond with children so they will want to do what we teach and model as being right. Secondly, although our emotional reaction should not be violent, it is OK to show emotional disappointment (when one child is cruel to another child, for instance). On the other hand, if we show frustration when the child is a slow learner, he/she may develop guilt over something that needs help rather than condemnation. Think about what leads you to show you are upset with a child. Is it more upsetting to you when a child turns over his punch on the floor, or when he cruelly teases a classmate ? Which is really more important ? And which could be classified as an accident, and thus need training rather than reproof ?

Experts used to say that teachers should refrain from teaching advanced concepts like patriotism and loyalty to children, as they think in terms of concrete objects and don't understand abstract concepts. Somehow we as Christians always knew that wasn't right, since the Bible says, "Train up a child in the way he should go and when he is old, he will not depart from it." (Prov. 22:6). But we often didn't understand how to begin teaching important concepts like kindness in the early years. Psychologists have now given us a clue. Young children may not think the way adults do, but their emotions are even more intense than adults' emotions. So, they can tie feelings of patriotism to that surging feeling inside when a parade comes by with a band playing "The Star Spangled Banner." We can call attention to how good it makes them feel when they do something kind for someone else. God made them that way. If you "catch them being good" and ask them how it makes them feel, they'll usually reward you with a big smile even before they have the words to describe the feeling. Then you can refer to, "Remember how you felt yesterday when you let Johnny use your new pencil with the eraser because he didn't have an eraser ? That's called being kind, and the good feeling you get is God's way of telling you that you're doing the right thing."

Thus emotions help children in two very different ways. Conscience and guilt cause children to refrain from doing what they shouldn't because of the unpleasant feelings that will follow. Good feelings about doing what is right, especially when pulled out and talked about by the teacher, will lead to what we call **altruistic behavior**: doing good things for others rather than remaining self-centered. Young children by nature are self-centered, and we need to be cognizant of that so we won't be too hard on this natural developmental tendency. However, since God loves us just the way we are, but also loves us too much to let us stay that way, we as teachers must love and accept our children but "woo" them into growing better morally.

Most early childhood classrooms that are under control have capitalized on one of two emotions: **fear or love.** Needless to say, those classrooms that are under control through love are happier classrooms. But why don't all teachers control through love, if that's better ? Probably because they equate love with being permissive, and a permissive classroom is **not** going to be under control. Children tend to "want what they want when they want it," and we have to help them see that, in order for the classroom to run smoothly, some of their wants have to give way to the wants and needs of others. Classrooms controlled by love must demonstrate the feeling that, "I love you too much to let you act that way."

Needless to say, the teacher must first demonstrate genuine warmth and love to the children through smiles, pats, nods, and words of encouragement. Otherwise the loving bond necessary for controlling through love will not be established. If children get the feeling that the teacher is basically irritated with them rather than enjoying and caring for them, they can become quite "sneaky" in going against the adult rules. On the other hand, the teacher who is loved (and preschoolers **want** to love you--this is much easier than in upper grades) can simply express how disappointed (not angry) she is in what a student has done, and the average preschooler will hang his head in shame. I have seen this happen many times--even to the point that the teacher frequently has to assure the child that, "It's OK. I know you're not going to do this again." If the child begins to develop a habit pattern of repeating undesired behavior, yet seems very ashamed after it happens, think through a way of building success. Just as you may teach a child a cue to help with reading, you may also teach cues to help with behavior. Help the child to recognize the feelings that lead to inappropriate behavior (those feelings, again, are the key) and suggest a better way to solve such problems before the emotions get out of hand. If the child has trouble recognizing the feelings, become a careful observer of behavior so that you can redirect the activities or say, "Johnny, remember?" when you see the symptoms developing. We want to teach for success in this area just as much as any important academic area like reading--perhaps even more. Remember, the Bible says, "A man without self control is like a city broken into and left without walls." (Prov. 25:28)

In addition, for those who are convinced that academic learning is the main thing children need in school, nothing will interfere with learning like uncontrolled behavior, both for the child himself and for others.

Although there are many other techniques for working effectively with preschool children, let's wait to talk about them within the context of specific academic areas or in the chapter that deals more in depth with classroom management skills. In the next chapter we'll look at the children as they emerge from these sensitive beginnings for learning into the important years that are sometimes called the "forgotten years." These are the years between early childhood and adolescence.

CHAPTER V

Ready for Formal Learning

**"And these words which I command you today shall
be in your heart. You shall teach them diligently to
your children, and shall talk of them when you sit
in your house, when you walk by the way, when you
lie down, and when you rise up." Deut. 6 :6 - 7**

The "Five-to-Seven Shift"

As previously mentioned, at the beginning of this next period of
development children go through a phenomenon known as the "five-
to-seven shift." This title has been given because of the tendency all
over the world to treat children of this age in a different manner than
they were treated before. Even primitive countries where they do not
count years or birthdays as we do, recognize children during this period
as progressing to a maturity where more can be expected of them.
Adults tend to give them more responsibility for self-care, as well as
family chores. The Catholic church has always recognized the child as
ready to study the catechism for progression to an adult faith. Organized
games also develop in importance.

The physical signals in the child that enable adults to make this
judgment, even in countries that do not count years of age, are the loss
of baby teeth and replacement by permanent teeth, the streamlining of
the body to lose baby fat and become more long-legged and lean, and
the increasing refinements of fine motor skills. Additionally, children
begin to be more able to reason problems through in the manner of an

adult. In varied and subtle ways, the parent-child relationship begins to change. Often by this time there are additional children born into the family which change the birth order position from being youngest to having others who need the assistance of the child himself.

The "Forgotten Years"

Psychologists sometimes refer to the years from six to around ten as the "forgotten years," because so much emphasis has been placed upon brain research and sensitivity of the preschool years, while the teenage years have also demanded much attention due to the unsettled behavior tumultuous hormones produce. Nevertheless, much of importance is occurring during this time period. Actually, while building on the foundation begun in the preschool years, this may be the "last chance" for the parent or teacher to impress major values and morals into the child before he becomes highly attuned to the influence of his peers. Similarly, from an academic standpoint this may be the most important period for impressing upon the child that school and learning are to be highly valued and that a responsible work ethic is a worthy goal.

A widely respected secular psychologist by the name of Erik Erikson has characterized this period as being one in which the child struggles with feelings of himself as showing **industry vs. inferiority.** In order to emerge from this period perceiving himself as a worthwhile individual, he must feel that he, at least most of the time, is successful in completing worthwhile "work." Otherwise, according to Erikson's research with children around the world, he will receive the message that he is inferior. Every teacher of children in the first grade, and frequently in kindergarten as well, is aware of how important a child's "work" is to him; that is to say, the papers he completes and takes home for his parents to review. And, by the way, these papers should be collected, put into some type of packet, and sent home to be signed by the parents at least once per week. This imbues the work with importance, and helps the child to do his best, while giving him something he truly can feel **industrious** to have accomplished. Every effort should be made to enable him to feel this sense of accomplishment, lest he begin to perceive himself as **inferior.** This means having high standards, but allowing the child to seek improvement in himself, not comparing himself with the achievements of others.

One of the teacher's major tasks during this period is to keep a sample of each child's work about every four weeks so that the comparison can be used to show the child his accomplishment. Children will, in spite of our best efforts, tend to compare themselves with each other. Although the Bible warns against this as unwise, it seems to be human nature to do so. The warning against such behavior in II Corinthians 10:12 states, "For we dare not class ourselves or compare ourselves with those who commend themselves. But they, measuring themselves by themselves, and comparing themselves among themselves, are not wise." Such comparisons invariably lead to feelings of inferiority or a puffed up false pride. When the child himself refers to some other child's work (either positively or negatively) as compared with his own, the teacher must point out that God has made each one of us as individual as snowflakes. Just as under a magnifying glass one can see that no two snowflakes or fingerprints are alike (a good example of a "teachable moment" science lesson for the children to experience), so God has planned each of us as specifically endowed key individuals in His world. If the opportunity presents itself (and yes, problems such as a child expressing himself to be inferior should be capitalized upon as an opportunity for help) , the teacher might say, "Yes, Johnny finds it easier to write a report than you do, but look how beautiful your artwork is (or how skillful you are with math facts, etc., etc.). And, look at this paper you wrote six weeks ago as compared to today's work. See how much progress you've made in organizing your thoughts (or keeping your margins even, etc., etc.)." Looking for the positives in each child in advance will enable the teacher to be an encourager in this manner. I recently attended a church camp's final program where my eight grandchildren, ranging in age from four to age twelve, were each presented with a medal to hang around their neck while their teacher told the major virtue she saw in this child. What an example that was of rewarding positive character traits with a tangible symbol! Even more importantly, these young teachers had known from the beginning of the week that they would be presenting these medals, so they had to remain alert to seek out the positive traits of each child in advance. What a powerful practice to improve both teacher and child! How often we tend to focus on the child's negatives to scold him, rather than on his merits to encourage him!

One way of looking at the developmental needs of these "forgotten years" is to look at the work done by an American psychologist named Robert Havighurst who coined the phrase "developmental tasks." He defined these tasks as being extremely important for children to master at specific stages of development because failure at these key tasks would lead to disapproval of society, unhappiness in the child, and difficulty in succeeding at the tasks required by later stages. Success, on the other hand, would lead to approval by society, a sense of accomplishment and well-being in the child, and the courage to approach future tasks with confidence. Sounds like these are pretty important things to help the child master, doesn't it ? Knowledge can be power when used in the correct manner. Proverbs 10:14 tells us, "Wise men store up knowledge." Similarly, Proverbs 3:13-14 says, "How blessed is the man who finds wisdom, and the man who gains understanding. For its profit is better than the profit of silver, and its gain than fine gold." Thus, an awareness of what specific tasks are crucial for the child to master in order that he can most effectively develop into all that God has planned for him, should be a great asset for the teacher.

One of the developmental tasks of middle childhood in our culture is a mastery of reading. Truly, the non-reader has little chance of continuing his formal education, as independent learning for the rest of his life will depend largely on his ability to seek out and read information on his own. Also, our society has an unfortunate disdain for the illiterate, and the child will thus suffer much disapproval if this task is not mastered, which will lead him to feeling inadequate and perhaps "stupid." No child of God should have to suffer from this label, whether it is adopted by himself or assigned to him by others! Therefore, every teacher should be a teacher of reading to those who are lagging behind in their mastery of the skill. The chapter on reading will give a variety of methods for doing this, based upon the child's learning style.

Another developmental task of this stage is mastering the group games (both physically and mentally) that are characteristic of this period, thus leading to acceptance by the child's peers. Much of this has to do with motor development and is a major reason why children

should not advance too far in school beyond their biological age group .
I can give a personal testimony in this area. When I was four years old,
the doctor told my mother that I needed to be in school because I had
no siblings or children in the neighborhood my own age. My mother,
not knowing about the existence of preschools (and also not being able
to drive), found out that a woman two blocks from our house had a
small first and second grade school in her home. She enrolled me, and
I learned to read at four years of age. When I was six years old, mother
took me to the public school, where my reading level was tested and I
was placed in the third grade. I could always keep up academically, but I
have many memories of always being the last one chosen for any athletic
game because my muscle coordination was two years behind the other
children (although I certainly didn't know that was the reason). Bearing
out what Havighurst said (although he had not even done his research
at that time), from that day to this I have always felt that proverbially I
could not "walk and chew gum"! Perhaps by nature I never would have
been skillful in this area, but for years I struggled with great feelings
of failure because of this experience, not only physically but also in my
peer relations in general.

Of most importance to the Christian educator is this stage's
developmental task of learning more about the importance of rules
and true morality. Children during the elementary years become very
group-game/competition oriented. In this context, they begin to realize
that the game cannot be played successfully unless everyone abides by
the rules. There seems to be an increasing awareness of the importance
of being "fair" to everyone. As a matter of fact, if a person visits an
elementary school playground, regardless of where it is located, he is
liable to hear wails of, "It's not fair!" Perhaps as parents you have also
encountered this same accusation. Scientific studies have indicated that
when a child is particularly "ripe" for a certain learning, he will tend
to center on it and desire to practice it. This fascination with game
rules and desire to understand what being "fair" is all about presents
the "teachable moment" for this part of morality. It is not that we don't
teach all kinds of morality as we go along, but if we take advantage of
the natural desire to learn during this period, it is more likely to become
vividly remembered. Children of this age, at first, will concentrate on

exact equality as being fair. Everyone must receive the same treatment and be judged by the same rules. As teachers, we need to model the essence of fairness so that children will want to follow us as role models. As the children become more mature in this concept, we will need to teach the concept of "equity" as being more fair than exact "equality." For instance, if a six-year-old is competing with a ten-year-old, some allowance may be made for their varying levels of skill in order to make it more "fair." Pull these concepts out and talk about them, or they probably will not be recognized and truly internalized. Ask the child, "Do you think I should give Johnny a 30-second head start on the race? Why or why not?" It will get them to thinking in less egocentric ways, which is one of the main goals of this stage.

Hey! What's Happening Here ?

Have you ever felt that maybe--just maybe--as parents or teachers we might be teaching our children something that we'd really rather that they **didn't** learn ? It happens all too often. The parent, eager to save some money on a movie ticket, casually says to her 12-year-old son or daughter, "Tell them you're eleven. You're small for your age--they won't know the difference." What a temptation ! Movie tickets are expensive, and why should a couple of months in age make such a difference ? But, in the process the child is learning that: 1) a lie is OK if it's really helpful; 2) money is more important than truthfulness; and 3) it's "smart" sometimes not to tell the truth. All that ?! I'm afraid so. So often, those things learned as "incidental learning" (the overall "feel" one gets for the situation, although it's not spelled out in so many words) tend to be internalized more completely than those that are directly taught (like the Sunday School lesson on being honest), and thus "incidental learning" can become "accidental learning," with disastrous consequences.

In the classroom, a similar rule applies. Children are frequently watching what we **do** so carefully they can't hear a word we say ! We tell them to keep up with their homework, emphasizing how this demonstrates the responsibility they need in their lives. But we, as teachers, may wait **weeks** to grade and return major test papers or themes, which they need to have as feedback on how to study for the next project. We tell them how important it is to read, but do they ever see us reading ? I once heard of a teacher who came into her fifth-grade classroom reading a book with great excitement. She sat down at her desk and continued to read. The tardy bell rang. She continued to read. Finally, a couple of students approached her. She said, "Don't bother me--I'm in the most exciting part of this book, and I just can't put it down !" The whole class was amazed, and talked of this strange phenomenon for days ! I'm not sure I'd be brave enough to try this myself, but she got a message across to her students, loud and clear--reading can be exciting !

In short, ask yourself what "incidental" learning is taking place in your classroom, and don't let it become "accidental." Avoid sending the wrong messages, and think through how you can honestly send messages that motivate learning. For instance, shortly after I came to university teaching I was asked to teach a methods class in Social Studies. This really worried me, because even though I am an enthusiastic learner in most areas, I had always disliked Social Studies. Since I know that attitudes are more "caught" than "taught," I didn't want to be a "wet blanket" for my students' enthusiasm for the subject. But on the other hand, I feel strongly that you can't pretend something you don't feel. Having dealt with students from kindergarten to college, I can assure you that any sense of falseness, even if it is mistakenly aroused, will destroy the trust and rapport your students have with you. So, I thought, in order to generate the enthusiasm each teacher must seek to pass along to her students for the subject, I must figure out how I could get excited about Social Studies! First of all, why didn't I like it? It is the study of people, after all, and I have always been fascinated by people. I decided that I had been the victim of poor teachers in this subject, in that I had always had to "read the material and answer the questions at the end of the chapter." What, then, would have made me excited about Social Studies?

To make a long story short, after carefully analyzing what could be exciting about this field of study, I ended up having student groups put together units about various countries, and in the process we transformed our room into an environment that taught the culture involved. One group turned the room into a Japanese tea room, covering the floor with blankets and serving a formal tea ceremony to the other students as we all sat on the floor. Another time, there was a huge river (complete with tall grasses along the bank which had been "harvested" from the lake near our campus) for which the students built a canoe to conduct us to our jungle destination. Another group had the chairs arranged as a jet airliner bound for our country, with a stewardess making announcements of what to expect upon landing, and showing an in-flight movie concerning our destination. For these and other countries studied, we sang, danced, ate ethnic food, and played games from the various cultures.

No, this wasn't the only thing we did. We also learned how to become interested in an area and then use research techniques to find out more about it, utilizing our presentation skills by presenting that information to the class. I realized that moral development, in the eyes of secular education, belongs in the field of Social Studies. That gives teachers the right to introduce it into a public school classroom. (As a matter of fact, I was able to emphasize the current awareness, even in secular circles, that moral development must return to the classroom in order to stem the tide of violence and disrespect for authority that is rampant in our schools today.)

I had as a major objective that my students would find out how much fun it is to be creative in teaching and learning about Social Studies, and that they would also learn that if **they** are excited about the subject, the children will be, too! And, in the process, I got really excited about teaching Social Studies ! I have pictures of some of the delightful ways my students and I learned together (which is the best way--our classes should always be "communities of learners," including the teacher !). To tell the truth, although I had originally resisted teaching this course, a few years later the assignment was given to another teacher, and I found myself mourning the loss of "one of my favorite classes"! I had built real, not simulated, enthusiasm for the course by "looking for the positives" !

What in the world is the "Teachable Moment"?

As we plan to take advantage of "incidental learning," as teachers we must be ever-vigilant to discover the "teachable moment." This means realizing that although we already have made careful plans about teaching the U.S. Constitution to our class, if an issue arises in the local newspaper or in the school lunchroom concerning the tendency of the strong to take advantage of the weak, now is the time to pull out the issue and discuss the implications for the students' lives. As they express their feelings on the issue and relate it to their lives, their higher-level thinking will be activated and they will be able to truly understand why our US Constitution was written. How often we pass up such God-given opportunities to help our students realize why school learning is important ! Also, because of the vividness of the tension-related event, research shows that they will retain the learning longer.

Similar in philosophy but with a differing outcome, you may have plans for the day that have little correlation with an exciting event. On a snowy day in Texas (which is a rare and spectacular occurrence), I have seen Kindergarten teachers simply draw the blinds and go on with "business as usual "! How much better it is to set aside at least part of the lesson for the day and have art work in which they draw snow scenes on dark blue construction paper with toothpaste (makes the whole room smell good, too !), talk about the individuality of each snowflake (relating it to how individually special each student is), and bundle out to the playground for long enough to look at a snowflake under a magnifying glass. The carefully planned lesson can be used another day, but the "teachable moment" of snow in Texas comes only rarely ! God gives us so many of these opportunities! We just need to pray for the sensitivity to notice and take advantage of them.

As we strive for the "teachable moment," we must remember what types of events particularly appeal to the age group we are teaching, and which events may disrupt certain needs of theirs at this time. Look back into previous chapters over the characteristics of your age group of concern, then plan to utilize these interests as a motivational "hook" to make learning real and exciting to them. For instance, preschoolers have a great need to be actively involved and moving about rather than spending too much time in just sitting; so the active approach to the snow is ideal. However, they also derive a great deal of their security from routines and in an ability to predict "what comes next" in the schedule. Therefore, it would be advisable not to eliminate all aspects of their usually scheduled routines. Elementary school children, with their need to feel that they have accomplished meaningful work, should be allowed to complete writing projects related to these vivid opportunities which occur spontaneously. They should also be encouraged to research more of their interests about the topic, with careful instruction on utilizing reference materials. The class might produce on chart paper a "KWL" chart. The teacher instructs them to tell her, as she writes it under the "K" column, what they already know about the topic. Next, under the "W" column, she should record what they would like to know about it (these can later be divided up for individual assignments). The "L" column should be reserved for the reports later about what they have learned.

Our key verse for this chapter, which is from Deuteronomy 6:6-7, gives some of the best advice available anywhere on effective teaching for both parents and teachers. Whatever is important for children to learn, you should **talk** about it when you **sit** in your house (or school room), when you **walk** by the way, when you **lie down**, and when you **rise up**. In other words, every moment of every day is a teaching moment for children. Take advantage of it, and pass this tip on to the parents, also. In their situations, many times the **walk** part may occur when taking children individually in the car to various ball games, music lessons, etc. I have learned with my own children that such bits of time represent an ideal opportunity for quality discussion and influence in our busy world.

CHAPTER VI

Reading--the Basis of Lifelong Learning

"...and it shall be with him and he shall read it all the days of his life , that he may learn to fear the Lord his God, by keeping all the words of this law and these statutes, and doing them;" Deut. 17: 19

We can give our children no greater gift for their future learning than the gift of a love for reading. Indeed, since our children will need to be lifetime learners in order to deal with this world of knowledge explosion, they must first learn to look upon reading as something they will continue to **choose** to do outside the walls of school.

Research shows that although there are many methods of teaching reading, some of which are more successful for certain types of learners and other methods which work best for others, there is one background element in successful readers that has proven to be universal. That is the fact that for some reason successful readers have come to associate reading with a pleasurable experience. In many cases, this can be traced back to a parent reading to the child at a very young age (often even before the infants can talk) by holding him on the parent's lap and showing love and warmth while reading. This experience is called the use of "lap books." What a great "tip" to pass on to the parents in our classrooms who have young babies! However, if that stage has already been missed, there are other ways to build that pleasure. Reading as a part of bedtime routines (for parents) and reading aloud interesting and developmentally appropriate books in the classroom **daily** (up through the eighth grade!) can begin the habit of pleasure in reading, or keep that pleasure going. For older children, it is especially desirable to read toward an exciting part of the book, then tell the children, "If you'd like to know what happens to _____, I'll put three copies of this book in our library center for you to check out and read for yourself." That's using the old "soap opera technique," but for their own good, in discovering the excitement and suspense of a good book

There is a great deal of controversy today concerning the "best" way to teach reading. The experts themselves cannot seem to agree. From a thirty-year background of experience in the field, I would like to advise you that if you become too thoroughly convinced that one method is best, you will hurt a lot of children. This is because children have different learning styles, and what works best for one will frequently not work at all for another. That is why a teacher should not be just a **technician**, who knows one method and applies it diligently to all children, but a **scholar** and **diagnostician,** who knows a variety of techniques and diagnoses the child for the proper prescription. Whole books are written on the teaching of reading, so I can only begin to touch on the subject, but perhaps I will be able to give you a few terms and hints which will lead you to seek out further reading elsewhere. Remember: you, just like your students, must prepare to be a lifetime learner if you want to be the blessing to your students God planned for you to be. If you ever think you "know it all" or have "arrived," you will not only be wrong, you will be failing to live up to the high calling of being a teacher.

There's More Than One Way To Skin a Cat !

One of the more controversial methods of teaching reading is related to whether or not to teach **phonics**. Phonics is a method of teaching reading which is based on the sound/symbol correlation of the language. Children are taught to memorize the primary sounds of each letter of the alphabet, then blend these sounds into words by "skating" from sound to sound.

The "positives" of this method include:

1. giving the child a way to attempt to "break the code" of reading,
2. helping the child have a sense of power over the printed word,
3. capitalizing on children's observed tendency as toddlers to use a certain degree of "natural phonics," which seems to "fit" naturally with the method.

The "negatives" of the method include:

1. English is one of the most irregular of all languages phonetically; there sometimes are more exceptions to phonetic rules than there are good examples of them;
2. Too much emphasis on analyzing the sounds can fragment the reading process, resulting in "barking at print" instead of reading for meaning;
3. A predominantly "worksheet approach" is frequently used, which robs the beginning reader of the joy of discovering good books.

A careful analysis of the strengths and weaknesses of utilizing phonics to teach reading will enable the dedicated teacher to capitalize on the strengths, while avoiding the possible pitfalls. One of the typical problems of the young child is a feeling of powerlessness in the daily process of coping with a world in which everyone seems to be bigger, stronger, and smarter than he is. Psychologists tell us that the feeling of powerlessness is one of the most difficult emotions in the world to endure. When you think about it, a young child must naturally feel that he is in a "land of the giants"! Accordingly, when children feel they are able to get a tool which gives them power over decoding the printed word, it is one step away from such a feeling of weakness and confusion. Let's help them have the power to make an "educated guess" at reading by teaching **the more regular** phonic rules, then letting them depend on the context of the story (more of this when we discuss the "whole language" approach) to figure out the rest. In short, the teaching of phonics is one weapon in the arsenal of equipment we will give children to help them feel successful in breaking the code and experiencing the joy of reading.

Another useful technique for reading instruction is the teaching of **sight words.** These are words that are usually not regular phonetically, but are used a large number of times in print. They are therefore sometimes called "high frequency" or "high utility" words. We teach children to recognize these words "on sight," both because it is counterproductive to try to analyze them phonetically (many are irregular phonetically, such as "the") and because it will help them to read more rapidly. This faster reading allows them to read for meaning, since concentration on only decoding slows the process until often all continuity of thought and meaning is lost. Much research has gone into just which words qualify for this list and in what order they should be taught, so the teacher does not need to figure this out alone. The *Dolch Basic Sight Word List* will be discussed here, but there are others.

An example of the importance of teaching sight words is shown on a table in *Diagnosing and Remediation of the Disabled Reader,* third edition, by Eldon E. Ekwall and James L. Shanker. This is a highly respected college text for training future teachers in working with struggling young readers. The table is a summary of research, and indicates that if children learn to recognize on sight only the first <u>ten</u> words in frequency, they will know 20% to 25% of the words they will encounter in reading (what a morale booster for the child who feels he can't read <u>anything</u>!). If they recognize the first <u>100</u> words in frequency, they will be able to read 60% to 65% of all the words they will encounter at any reading level!

The *Dolch Basic Sight Word List* is a highly researched, well respected source for determining which words to teach. These should be broken down into groups of ten (or not over twenty, if your class is needing more challenge) words to teach for <u>instant</u> recognition before going on to the next list. Your class can be tested, individually or in groups, to see which list of sight words (always beginning with the simplest, most frequently occurring list) they can instantly recognize with 100% accuracy. Two errors (non-recognition or slow recognition of words) on the list indicate a child's instructional level. Then, when he shows instant recognition for <u>all</u> the words, he is ready to progress to the next group of sight words. Flash cards are the best way to teach or test when, as in this case, we seek instant recognition. Once children have been diagnosed for their instructional level, they each could have a set of cards to "keep" and paste on poster board for their own "word bank" to help them in writing.(Thank Heaven for this day of computer and copy-machine generated teaching aids!) These may be offered as a "prize" for each child after he or she has shown instant recognition of the words in that list.

Memorizing words can be dry and dull, or it can be made into a game. Anything as repetitive as this should not be continued for long periods of time, as it becomes boring. However. utilizing flash cards and having the children see how quickly they can "chorus" the word during those times of waiting in line to go to lunch, the playground, or when class finishes a little early, is a great use of time which otherwise would be wasted. Although waiting in line may only be five minutes, it still can lead to discipline problems, so you are really preventing problems while increasing "time on task." In addition, research has proven than several short periods of skill-drill rehearsal are more effective than one long period, as the monotony of lengthy repetition causes students to be less attentive.

Another technique for teaching reading is the use of **word analysis skills**.

This capitalizes on the awareness of root words, prefixes, and suffixes to divide the words into manageable amounts of material to be decoded, along with units of meaning that can be depended upon to change words in certain ways. Although it is not a complete method of teaching reading, it is a good auxiliary method, having the particular strength that both phonics and meaning are involved in the method.

All of the techniques mentioned to this point are in the philosophical school of the **bottom up** or **skills** approach to teaching reading. This means the print on the page is emphasized, along with specific skills that isolate the letters and other symbols while applying certain rules to them. As we teach the skills involved, hopefully the student will emerge with true reading.

The philosophical approach that is at the opposite end of the spectrum in the teaching of reading is the **top down** or **whole language** approach. In this process, the overall joy of reading and the patterns of language are emphasized, teaching the child to predict what is coming next, primarily based upon meaning rather than on specific skills. Here is a brief description of the techniques involved with this approach.

Experience charts are a **top down** example of allowing children to do something vivid and exciting (such as a field trip to a dairy farm), then recall their experience by dictating to the teacher what they have done. The teacher writes their retelling on a large chart, usually on lined paper, that is large enough for the entire class to view the letters and words as she forms them. In the process, the teacher leads the class to understand **sequencing**, as she asks for what happened first, next, last, etc. **Process** is also taught as it occurs. The teacher calls attention to the fact that she always starts on the left and moves to the right, then returns to the left at the end of the line. The fact that sentences start with a capital letter and end with a period also can be emphasized quite naturally in the process, as can any part of the process of reading/writing that the teacher chooses. This is an example of the "top down" approach in that it starts with an idea or experience that is then committed to writing, emphasizing the **meaning** rather than the **structure** of reading. One of the greatest strengths of the method, in my opinion, is the fact that as many of the **skills** can be taught as desired, but in a very natural way as they occur. The primary purpose is still to commit an exciting activity to print and then to be able to relive it by reading about it. After the children have finished dictating the story, the teacher leads them through reading the story together. They read the story as a group many times, with the teacher pointing to each word as it is read, making sure that all eyes are on the printed words as they read. She then calls on individual children to read specific words or sentences. After considerable **group guided practice** the chart can be cut apart into sentence strips to be studied and read individually and then reassembled. Although much of the reading may, at first, be memory (young children are extremely good at memorizing), careful emphasis on the visual aspect of the reading causes sight word recognition to develop.

It is impossible to overemphasize the importance of reading good books aloud to the children. This is also an example of the **top down** or **whole language** approach to reading because it capitalizes on ideas, meaning, and the joy of language and reading. Books should be chosen which are appropriate to the children's interest level, but perhaps somewhat above their ability to read by themselves. This will draw them into reading books that are somewhat more difficult than they would usually choose, for interest is a powerful motivation for curiosity and success in "growing" as a reader. If the students in your class seem to be interested in reading only comic books, remember that this is still reading, and don't "put them down" for it. On the contrary, gradually introduce comic books of a higher quality, then books with many pictures but lots of action, and gradually read aloud to them books that will whet their desire for getting into more appropriate (but still exciting and humorous) books on their own. Remember--the reading interests with which a student **comes** to your class are the teacher's **opportunity**. The reading interests with which a student **leaves** your class are the teacher's **responsibility**.

A number of concepts are utilized in the **top down** or **whole language** approach to the teaching of reading. I'd like to acquaint you with some of the terminology, with brief examples of how this works. First of all, **emerging literacy** is currently emphasized, as opposed to the previous concept of **reading readiness**. In **reading readiness**, the emphasis is on teaching the child the skills necessary for reading, such as recognition of likenesses and differences in print, phonics, etc., and in waiting until the child is developmentally ready for such instruction. In **emerging literacy**, the realization is that the child is beginning the process of becoming literate from the moment he begins to experience the print around him and scribble on paper with crayons. He learns to write as he learns to speak--by being surrounded with language, wanting to send a message of his own, and through trial and error accomplishing this.

An important component of this "top down" method is teaching children to read for meaning by utilizing what they already know from past experiences. Children develop **schemata**, or background experiences, that help them to make sense out of their world. As teachers, we want to encourage them to use these **schemata**, this previous knowledge, to learn to read and write. As we encourage their higher-level-thinking skills to analyze what they already know and use it to help them in this new situation, we provide **scaffolding.** A scaffold is a temporary structure for holding a building secure during its construction or repair until the building is stable enough to support itself alone. Similarly, the **scaffolding** of this type of reading instruction is a temporary assistance until the child is able to succeed on his own. The teacher provides no more support than is necessary to prevent failure, as the child constructs his own process of learning to read based on what "fits" best with his natural learning style. An important concept here is a term coined by Lev Vygotsky called the **zone of proximal development**. This is a description of how much a child can accomplish with the assistance (scaffolding) of an adult, as compared with how much he can accomplish without help. The role of the adult is to find out when to help, and how much, with the emphasis upon leading the child to increasingly complex tasks, but with the ultimate goal of self-sufficiency. Our Lord has set us an example in that He died for us, providing the forgiveness we did not deserve and could not attain on our own. Yet He has also sent us the "Comforter," the Holy Spirit, to gradually aid us as we seek to follow Him. He didn't expect us to do it totally on our own, but has the ultimate goal of maturing us into the followers of Christ that we were designed to be.

Another key technique in the whole language approach to the teaching of reading is the use of **Journaling** . Children are given specific questions to answer, or they are allowed free choice of subjects about which to "journal." . This may be used as an early morning "sponge" activity while other children are arriving (the term "sponge" is used because these activities can absorb more or less time, depending on what is needed) which routinely occurs every day, or it may be a specially scheduled event to write about something the children have experienced (sort of like individual **experience charts**). The theory behind this relates to the whole language concept that writing and reading should be allowed to develop together, just as listening and speaking do.

When the child is too young to actually write his thoughts down, he draws a picture to record those thoughts in his journal. The teacher circulates to each child helping him to write down what has been communicated. At first, the teacher may take the child's dictation and print it in manuscript at the bottom of the picture, but gradually through questioning, "hints for success" and "guessing" at how to produce the symbols needed, the child is encouraged to commit his message to print. It is important at this point not to be critical of a child's efforts, or he will not continue to try. Certainly, as babies begin to speak, even though their mother may be the only one able to understand those first words, we all smile, encourage, and applaud their early attempts, however flawed they may be. Similarly, early attempts at spelling with **natural phonics** will not be at all what would be desired for the final product. Research has shown that children go through fully predictable stages of writing as they emerge into literacy. For instance, they use **letter name spelling** (There is a delightful children's book called *CDB?* (stands for "See the Bee?") by William Steig that illustrates this developmental stage of spelling. They go through a very natural tendency to think letters should sound phonetically like the letter name, even when the connection seems more farfetched than *CDB.* For instance, children who are trying to spell "once" for "once upon a time" frequently start the word with a "w". Think about it. "Once" does sound like it begins with a "w!" Naturally, you don't want them to continue to spell this way, but you don't want a baby to continue talking unintelligible baby talk, either. You encourage beginning production of both speech and writing without criticism, then gradually shape both into specific improvements.

Whether you are working with a three-year-old and trying to encourage his natural development of love and skill in reading and writing, or with a teenager who is still reading at a second grade level, you are, in a sense, "teaching reading." However, the techniques must vary considerably. We must learn to fit the techniques to the child's natural motivation by remembering to remain developmentally appropriate. Why do we insist on trying to make children into something God never intended for them to be at certain ages ? If He had wanted them to arrive on this earth thinking like an adult, surely He could have managed that! There must be a purpose for the developmental characteristics of each age, and therefore wise is the teacher who seeks out those characteristics and uses them to make reading (or any other subject) exciting !

For the three-year-old, for example, the task must be play oriented, with much individual freedom to get up and move around as needed. Did you know that since preschoolers' muscles and long bones are developing so rapidly, requiring them to sit for long periods may actually be painful to many ? They need an opportunity to stretch those developing muscles. On the other hand, it has been found that sometimes very young children can remain quiet and "on task" for as long as 45 minutes when it is a <u>self chosen</u> activity. Montessori, who is deeply respected for her philosophy and methods with young children, felt that the future teacher should be instilled with the self-sacrificing spirit of the disciple of Christ and the observational skills of the scientist. (Yes, she was a devout believer herself in Christ, which many non-believing Montessori teachers choose to ignore!) With this background, she felt the teacher should then go to the child himself, observe him, and sacrificially adjust her teaching methods accordingly, thus learning to teach. Just as we should teach our children to observe and analyze life, then utilize problem-solving skills, we as teachers must do the same. As we strive to become the "self-sacrificing disciples of Christ," rather than trying to make children learn by <u>our</u> favorite methods, we should observe what "works" for them. In order to be able to do this, we must familiarize ourselves with many ways to teach the subject, and then <u>individualize</u> . Scripture says, "Let each of you look not only to his own interests, but also to the interests of others." Phil. 2:4

For the teenagers still reading on a second grade level, although we know that people best "learn to read by reading" (a favorite phrase of Frank Smith, key reading expert), we also know that such teenagers will not tend to do much reading ! Which one of you, when you have experienced nothing but failure all day in an area that is forced upon you, would go home and choose it for your free time? There might be a few of you that are that self-disciplined, but probably not many. And I guarantee you there are even fewer teenagers in that category! So, how do we **motivate** these teens to read ? Remember, **motivation** is defined as creating a need or a desire for something in an individual that will lead him to do something to fulfill that need or desire. In other words, we've all heard the old saying, "You can lead a horse to water, but you can't make him drink." That is, of course, the problem.

You can expose a child to reading, but you can't make him read. So, what can you do with this proverbial horse? You can feed him salt! That makes him <u>want</u> to drink. It <u>motivates</u> him ! What about the teenager? Find out his hobbies. Does he like to build model airplanes? Get some models for the classroom and help him see how reading the instructions can help him do a better job. Does he like to repair cars? Get some magazines on cars and keep them in the classroom. Is he a member of the football team? Get a book on key plays. These may be the "salt" that will create a desire to read. Then <u>you</u> will be there to provide the <u>scaffolding</u> to lead him to success in reading when he wants to find out information in his area of interest. Girls may be interested in grooming tips or "romance" stories. The key is to find out the interests, provide the materials, and be there to help! A delightful children's book called *Did You Carry the Flag Today, Charlie?* tells how a young teacher aroused a boy's interest in learning to read by observing his avid interest in learning more about snakes! One of an effective teacher's most important skills (often not cultivated) is in observing her students for information about situations like this.

A skilled teacher of reading learns to draw from both ends of the philosophical spectrum described in this chapter in order to teach reading. "Bottoms up" skills will be taught to enable the child to "break the code," combined with a "top down" use of encouraging delight in reading and writing about life itself. The amounts of each method used will be carefully diagnosed and prescribed for the learners, based on an awareness of their past experiences (including success or failure with certain techniques), their ages, and the situation involved. Students suffer when teachers stubbornly insist upon only teaching one type of reading instruction (their own particular favorite). Always remember that the effective teacher does not handle every student in identically the same manner, but reads constant feedback on the technique chosen, varying the technique if it does not seem to be appropriate.

Chapter VII

Writing As a Parallel for Reading

**"Nevertheless, brethren, I have written more boldly
to you on some points, as reminding you, because of
the grace given to me by God." Romans 15 : 15**

We have already mentioned the parallel development of reading and writing. Just as the young child learning to speak combines the skills of <u>listening</u> and <u>speaking</u> to help him better develop his communication skills, <u>writing</u> similarly feeds into the development of <u>reading</u>. Just as listening and speaking are the opposite ends of the same process and both are necessary for communication, the same is true for reading and writing. As we concentrate on the fact that the baby desires to learn to speak because he wants to **communicate,** we find the key for helping children to learn to read and write. Remember that we must often be the ones to <u>create</u> that need, or we may be out of luck ! When I was a little girl, my Daddy, of whom I was very fond, worked "early nights" at Western Union. This meant he worked from 3:00 P.M.. until 11:00 P.M.. Therefore in the mornings, while I was awake, he was still sleeping. When I went down for my nap, he got up and dressed for work; when I woke up, he was gone. Of course, when he came home after midnight, I was again asleep. This was very disappointing to me, for I loved my Daddy very much, and I wanted to at least <u>communicate</u> with him. I had a very wise mother who came upon a good plan. Every evening we would fix a sack lunch for my Daddy and put it in the refrigerator for him to have a "snack" when he got home. I would write "notes" to him to put in the sack. My mother saved a few of these, and they were crudely lettered, misspelled messages that sometimes (when I ran out of room at the end of the line) would cycle back around from right to left. What a mess ! But, I was striving to communicate, and my mother didn't stifle that by telling me all about what was wrong with my messages. She let my natural need to communicate develop into producing letters that could later be "cleaned up" to proper standards . The result was that I have always loved reading and writing, which has caused me to enjoy being a lifetime learner to the extent that I obtained my doctoral degree in formal education several years ago, and that has in no way become an "end point" to my learning.

"In the beginning..."

One reason very young children may only put down one or two letters to represent each word is because their fine motor skills are so poor that they must labor long and hard over each letter. They therefore find that their mind can work much faster than their fingers can cooperate, and rush on to the next word or thought. The handy phrase "tell me about it" comes in handy to help parents and teachers interpret these beginning communications, but at times a very young child may be trying to imitate adults who are sending a message, without having a specific message of his own. In these cases, he may bring you a paper with various forms of scribbling, some letter-like in formation and some not, and say, "What did I write?" In these cases, the adult can gently but kindly inform the child that although this looks like writing, for somebody else to read it the message has to have a special form. Then, if the child seems interested, show him or her how to write a short word or message, talking about the sounds of each letter.

A good place to start teaching writing is with the child's name--almost all children are motivated to learn to write (and recognize) their own names first. Be aware, however, that some names are much harder (and more subject to reversals) than others. For instance, growing up with the name "Sylvia" was not too easy ("S" is the letter most frequently reversed, even for older children). It's a good idea to help children realize this difficulty if their name is long or they struggle with particular letters. Encouragement is what is needed here, for parents as well as children, who are also eager for their child to be the "best and the brightest." Along these same lines, it's good to know (and to pass on to parents) that reversals of letters are quite common around four and five years of age. Some children even pass through a stage where they write everything as if it were a mirror image. Experts aren't exactly sure why this occurs, but one theory has to do with the two halves of the brain producing mirror images and the wrong image being delivered at certain developmental stages (around four or five). When I taught kindergarten, I found that most of the children who showed this characteristic tried to write from right to left. I would put a star in the top left-hand corner of their paper where they were to start. If they started there, they couldn't go from right to left, and I found that when they were thus forced to write from left to right their handwriting would no longer be in a mirror image. I don't know why this was true, but it worked for me, and it is something you might try.

Actually we don't begin to worry about a child being dyslexic unless the reversals persist until age seven. Unfortunately, a lot of parents (and teachers) don't know this, and they begin to make such an issue about reversals and having the child tested, etc., that they become victims of a "self-fulfilling prophecy." Because there is such an expectation to find abnormality, the child simply lives up to expectations. How much better it is to assume it is a normal stage, try a few simple techniques like I described, and know that if there is really a problem seven is not too late to begin testing and special programs for reversals (there's a lot of controversy about whether these work, anyway).

"...and the child grew in wisdom..."

Sometime around the third grade (this can frequently occur earlier in schools where children have had good background experiences, and it may need to be later for disabled readers), a new phase of writing development occurs. After a child has been encouraged to develop communication skills, writing to communicate without much mention of form, the time will come when it is a natural process for the adult to help him discover that unless everyone uses the same form, communication itself may not take place. Also, this is the time to begin the subtle process of hinting that people may judge us by the neatness and correctness of our writing. And if it is not neat and correct when they receive the message, they may doubt the intelligence or wisdom of the person sending it, and therefore not tend to give the message itself much credibility. This is "unfair," (middle elementary students are supersensitive to issues of fairness, so this would be a good time to bring up the concept), but we must live in the world the way that it is, not the way it ought to be. Even Christ, although He came to change the world forever, used an awareness of things that were happening around Him (many of which He certainly didn't approve) to illustrate His truths. Similarly, although all riches rightfully belong to God, He operated within the world's flawed structure by telling the people to look at the coin, see Caesar's image, and then to "render unto Caesar the things that are Caesar's, and unto God the things that are God's" (Matt. 22:21) Thus it is necessary for us to explain to children that, in order to reach the world, we must have the high standards that make the world respect our message, even though their judgments of our wisdom may be unfair.

From this point of writing instruction and on into the upper grades, in order to help students become effective communicators it is necessary to spend much time modeling the process. Talk about what _you_ do when you are about to write a letter, describe an experience, write a persuasive speech, or give a devotional. Then "create" the process for them on an experience chart (lower grades) or an overhead (upper grades), "talking your way through" the process, and later having the children "talk you through" what to do next.

" I hear, and I forget; I see, and I remember; I do, and I understand."

In addition to modeling the process for your students, it will be necessary, in order for their learning to be most effective, for them to be actively involved. All research on learning agrees that in order for learning to take place and be retained it is necessary for students to _do_ what they are learning rather than just _hear_ about it. As a matter of fact, some Socony Mobil research was conducted a number of years ago concerning how much (or little) people remember three days later of material that had been presented to them by various methods. The researchers were curious to find out how much people could remember <u>three days later</u> concerning material that they had learned by various methods. The results are shown on the chart below.

Method	Percentage Remembered
Read	10%
Hear	20%
See	30%
See and Hear	50%
Say Out Loud	70%
Do	90%

This goes along with the old Chinese proverb which says, "I <u>hear,</u> and I forget; I <u>see,</u> and I remember; I <u>do,</u> and I understand." Therefore, get your students involved in the pre-writing planning by giving them a topic and then letting them **brainstorm**. In brainstorming, children are free to call out suggestions, information, questions to be pursued, etc. just as it surfaces in their minds <u>without fear of being laughed at </u>! It is important to "set the ground rules" carefully before starting this process, indicating that in the creative process we must all be free to "playfully entertain" ideas that may seem too unimportant or foolish to mention. Many times these very thoughts can lead to new and creative problem-solving that otherwise would not have ever been considered. Therefore, it is <u>absolutely forbidden</u> to laugh at anything another student submits in brainstorming. A good motivation for this (using different terms depending on the ages of the students involved) is to ask them (in advance) whether they think they are mature ("grown up") enough to use this process, for it requires enough self control to avoid laughing at others' contributions. Certainly, when brainstorming is complete, we are going to pursue those ideas which seem to be leading most in the direction of the original goals for the writing, although others may be used later. Help the students to become aware that as one person makes a contribution it may lead another student to come up with an idea not previously considered, leading yet a third or fourth student to arrive at the goal-related concept. Thus, "Iron sharpens iron, and one man sharpens another." (Prov. 27:17)

As the students begin to work on their individual papers, it is important to be acceptant of spelling errors, incomplete sentences, and general disorganization, as they "get their ideas down on paper" before they forget them. However, they must realize that although the creative process may be messy and disorganized at first, it is <u>not</u> the final form. A good term for these beginning papers is for them to refer to this form as their **"sloppy copy."** (This is easy to remember, as children love the rhyme and the "upbeat" nature of the term.) I once had a young mother in our church express to me her extreme displeasure in the use of this new method of teaching writing, as it did not place proper emphasis on spelling, grammar, and other proper format in writing, but put all the emphasis on creativity. Her son had come home with a paper full of misspelled words and grammatical errors, with an "A" grade at the top. When she suggested that he needed to clean up the errors, he said to her, "You see that A? I don't need to do <u>anything</u> to this paper!" No wonder that mother was upset ! And, how sad it is that teachers are sometimes pressured into incorporating the "new" methods before they truly understand what needs to be included! A paper is not ready for a letter grade until it is in the final stage. Let's discuss the process of getting it there.

First of all, some of these "sloppy copies" may not be carried all the way through the process, for it <u>is</u> time consuming and should be reserved for those ideas which are really important and well developed. But a certain number of them should be required for completion by each child (depending upon the grade level and writing ability of the class, and perhaps adjusted for specific students' abilities within the class). This should be accomplished by some variation of the process below.

The teacher should make <u>encouraging comments</u>, not give letter grades, concerning the ideas and development of the **first draft/sloppy copy**. Suggestions can also be given concerning mechanical errors, with the very young receiving, perhaps, the correct spelling of word, etc. on their papers. But the ultimate goal should be to <u>mark</u> those areas needing attention and then expect the student to research correcting them himself. This process is the stage of **editing and proofreading.** It can be partially accomplished, as the grades progress, by allowing students to qualify to serve on "proofreading boards" that will work with the individual students in correcting their papers. First of all, this gives positive reinforcement for being good at the mechanical skills, thus rewarding careful writing with an <u>academic</u> reward rather than candy, stickers, etc. The more we can use as rewards such academic experiences as being on a proofreading board, getting a crossword puzzle "challenge," representing the class at a school wide spelling bee, etc., the more those "prizes" will establish (through that "incidental learning" we discussed earlier) that academic endeavors are both enjoyable and worthwhile.

After the chosen papers have been through the editing and proofreading process, the final copy is called the **published copy** or **"neat sheet."** This may take several rewritings in some cases, which will require much encouragement, <u>not</u> censure, from the teacher. At this point, there are several motivations for helping the children to see that all their work has been "worth it." Computers make **desktop publishing of student books** and **classroom newspapers** so much easier than they used to be, and what an incentive for the young author to see his actual work published in print! In the lower elementary grades, after such publishing occurs it is a further motivation to have the "young author" sit in the **author's chair,** a simple chair so labeled, have his classmates gather in a circle on the floor around him, and allow him to read his published work to the others. For older children, the teacher might tell about how C.S. Lewis, the well-known Christian author who wrote *The Narnia Series,* belonged to a group of writers called "The Inklings." These men met regularly and discussed ideas they had in progress, reading their work to each other. Similarly, small groups of students with interests in common could meet to discuss their ideas and progress.

Preparation of a carefully edited copy should also be encouraged for communicating with **pen pals,** another highly motivating activity. **Classroom thank you notes** and **letters of inquiry** concerning topics the class is researching also provide highly motivating reasons to "make this letter something we can be proud of."

Everything centers around helping children realize that writing is a necessary and interesting activity, rather than just a series of "fill in the blank"activities to be trashed as soon as turned in to the teacher for a grade.

CHAPTER VIII

Math--Measuring and Quantifying God's World

**"For which of you intending to build a tower,
does not sit down first and count the cost, whether
he has enough to finish it." Luke 15:28**

Now that we've touched on the first two of the proverbial "three R's" ("readin' and ritin'") it's time for the third major component for the foundation of all learning-- " 'rithmatick". On these three foundation stones rest the child's future attempts to be a lifetime learner. Without knowing how to read, write, and compute sums, how can he ever hope to continue to investigate the knowledge explosion that exists in our world today, or to study the wisdom of the ages without having to "reinvent the wheel" ? As our forefathers knew long before us, these are the tools most essential for equipping our children to learn, for with these they can continue to pursue knowledge long after we are no longer with them.

First impressions "set the stage."

As we start out with introducing our children to the world of math, their natural curiosity motivates them to be excited about a "hands on" approach to learning about their environment. Jean Piaget, perhaps the greatest educational genius of the past century, has defined the first two years of a child's life as the **"Sensory Motor Stage."**

This is because a child starts out learning all things by either using one of his five **senses** (hearing, seeing, touching, tasting, smelling) or by **manipulating it with his muscles** to see the result. Although some levels of understanding abstractions, such as one object representing another, are added to those tools during the third year, the sensory motor methods of learning continue to be the most effective and permanent ways of learning throughout the entire elementary school years. Actually, since the more vivid the learning is the better it is retained, the method is probably still best even for adults. Which way do you learn and remember the best--hearing a lecture on how to sew a dress, or actually being led through the cutting of the fabric, pinning, sewing, etc. that is required while you do the work yourself? But with a very young child, there is no choice if learning is to be effective.. Piaget has said that young children must "construct their own knowledge." If we just "talk at them" they may be able to "parrot back" things we have said, but they probably won't be able to really use the knowledge unless they actually experiment with it in a manipulative, "hands on" manner.

Jerome Bruner, another authority on education, has described an important concept called the **"spiral curriculum."** What this means in simple terms, is that a child begins to learn the foundation of advanced concepts at a very early age. For example, he learns what is developmentally appropriate for his eventual knowledge of rocket science in those preschool years. What ? Well, let's pull that out and look at it. Does the rocket scientist need to understand shapes and their relationship to each other ? That's where it all begins, isn't it ? The reason Bruner calls this the **"spiral curriculum"** is because each time a concept is reintroduced when the child is a little older, we cycle around and teach the concept in a bit more depth and detail, utilizing what has been previously taught. So Bruner's work had a big impact on the world during the 50's and 60's in realizing just how important those early years are for creating a foundation for future learning in our rocket scientists. As a matter of fact, he made these announcements about the time that Sputnik struck terror into the hearts of Americans for fear that the Russians would beat us to space and thus control the world. This fear was the major thing that led to the founding of Head

Start, an effort to get our children into the right educational mode at an early age. You've probably heard the expression, "A mind is a terrible thing to waste." Benjamin Bloom, during that same period, came out with a statement based on his research that 50% of a child's capacity for learning was in place by age four, and an additional 30% by age eight ! That really got everyone's attention! Though in the intervening years many educational theorists have tried to indicate that Bruner actually overstated the importance of the early years, current brain research seems to prove that he was, if anything, modest in his claims.

So, how do we go about preparing those young scientists of the future for their mathematical foundation ? We've already said they need to use manipulative materials. What types of things are appropriate to teach them ? Certainly an awareness of numerals (the written sign) and numbers (the concept they represent) is needed. This does <u>not</u> mean just teaching them to count. Many children come to preschool rattling off numbers at top speed, but have no idea what "two" cups or "five" napkins mean. And it's in those real life contexts that such learning takes on meaning. If we have eight preschoolers and only six cookies, we've got a real problem! If this happens, talk about it and get their input on what should be done. Some of their suggestions may well surprise you, and I'm sure you'll get a lot of laughs out of it. ("A merry heart doeth good like a medicine." Prov. 17:22 As a teacher of young children, you'll either learn to laugh at a lot of things, or you'll cry a lot. Choose laughter!) Have the children count out the cups with you for snack time. As they learn to say "one" as you put down the first cup, then wait to say "two" until the next cup is placed on the table, they are mastering an important mathematical concept known as **one to one correspondence**. This is one of the most basic concepts to the understanding of all math.

Shapes are another key concept for preparing those young rocket scientists. Before a person can learn to deal with ellipses and orbital consistencies, he must become aware of circles, ovals, and other basic shapes. Young children learn best about these by handling puzzle pieces in these shapes, cutting out and eating cookies baked in various shapes, and molding play dough into such shapes, both two dimensional and three dimensional. Before children learn to write and recognize names of their groups (for center and group assignments), symbols can be utilized to indicate their groups, telling them where they should go for the next part of the schedule. These groups may simply be represented as the "red square" group or the "yellow triangle" group. The symbol can then be hung on a planning board for the centers desired. The children thus are enabled to come into the classroom, and independently find their own work stations. This not only accomplishes the task of getting children smoothly into the small group and individual work stations where preschool learning takes place most effectively, but also boosts the child's feeling of self control in being able to be independently responsible for finding his own spot without adult assistance. Of course, the adult is always there to assist those needing help; but again we need to remember that we are **scaffolding**, providing only as much help as will be necessary for the child to become independent soon. In other words, the kindest thing we can do for our children as teachers is to "work ourselves out of being needed" (which is really only partially true, for we then will be beginning to form the **scaffolding** for the next task).

Sizes are another key concept to be developed in the young child. Our forefathers have known that for years, and the classic fairy tales that have endured from the oral tradition for centuries frequently embody the natural way to teach sizes--by comparison. Remember the big chair for Papa Bear, the middle-sized chair for Mama Bear, and the teeny-tiny chair for Baby Bear ? If you think about it carefully, you'll think of dozens of other examples. That is one reason why those classic fairy tales have endured for so many hundreds of years--they accomplished something adults wanted (teaching concepts and morals to children) in a way that was developmentally appropriate, and therefore worked! Use those fairy tales, emphasizing the concepts they teach. Let the children act out the story after they have heard it many times and tell you whether they are pretending to be big, little, or medium sized. For another method, we can help children to learn **classification** skills by allowing them to sort buttons, shapes, or other objects into large, medium, and small sizes.

In the paragraph before this one, it became evident that we need to teach not only **concepts**, but also mathematical **processes.**

Classification is one of those processes just described. **Seriation**, or the ability to place things in a series from large to small, etc. is another process taught in much the same way. Young children naturally love to place things in order from large to small, dark to light, etc. Again, this is a developmental characteristic that Piaget called **functional assimilation**, which simply means that when a child is developmentally ready for a learning, he loves to practice doing it over and over again. Remember, Montessori has given us the hint that as we watch the child he will show us what he is ready to learn and how to go about teaching it. A child that seems "hung up" on repeating some specific type of learning activity usually has a need to be doing this. It may be that the practice is necessary for the learning to become permanent. On the other hand, sometimes it is due to family or other problems or to his own temporary illness, causing the child to need the security of repeating a comfortable, already well-known process rather than tackling a new one. In any event, we should be very cautious about rushing a child into giving up the repetition of a learning activity that he seems hesitant to leave. Montessori, who has the reputation of having taught children to read at an earlier age than almost any other educational figure (even being successful in teaching this skill to retarded children), was a great respecter of this type of choice in children. All of her materials had to be introduced and explained to children before each child was permitted to work with them. When she felt a child had practiced long enough with a previous manipulative and was ready to experience something new, the teacher would approach him and say, "May I introduce you to the (pink tower for example) today ?" If his reply was, "No," Montessori (or her teacher trainee) would quietly put away the new manipulative and wait a few days before trying again. Remember, she knew that from the child himself she could best learn how to teach him, and she greatly respected his decisions about his own readiness to take on new material.

Problem solving is a key process that must be begun in early childhood. Just as young children must access previous knowledge to help them learn to read naturally, they can also be encouraged to do the same thing in working out mathematical problems of **spatial** relationships (What do we do if too many people are in the center, or if the doll is too big for the doll bed ?), **temporal** relationships (What shall we do when all of you want a turn at fire painting and it is only ten minutes before time to go home ?), and **division/sharing** situations (How can we see that all get a fair share, since there is not enough here for everyone to get a full piece ?) The latter, of course, combines a social/moral problem with a mathematical one. The exciting thing here is the fact that life is like that--it does not divide down "neatly" into issues of only one subject. And thus we must teach in an integrated fashion, just as it will be utilized in real life.

Building on that firm foundation...

As a child emerges from the "early years" (which are considered by "experts" to continue up until about the third grade), he becomes able to deal with learning in a way that Piaget describes as **concrete operations**. This means that, while children still do not think exactly like adults, they are beginning to be able to learn more advanced concepts and hold more than one such concept in mind at once. Thus they know that sometimes two different characteristics (such as height and width in a glass) both affect the overall volume. Up until the age of **concrete operations,** Piaget found, through his research with children from all over the world, that the child could only hold <u>one</u> such concept in mind at a time (usually the one most visually obvious), a characteristic known as **centration**. This, along with several other differences in the way the **pre-operational** child (Piaget's term for children from ages two until about seven years of age) thinks, makes it difficult (if not totally inadvisable) to strive to teach such concepts as subtraction and multiplication to a very young child. Although current-day theorists tend to think that children can sometimes grasp certain concepts at an earlier age than Piaget had thought possible, these "neo-Piagetians" as they are called recognize that there is too much of value in Piaget's research to "throw out the baby with the bath water" and completely abandon his teachings. This is just one more example of how teachers must remain lifetime learners in order to determine what is the latest, research-based finding to facilitate their teaching. Although knowledge is growing and awareness is changing, it is always best to not throw out what has worked in the past until we have found that the newer way is, indeed, better. On the other hand, it is equally important that we not become rigid and unwilling to look at new issues and methods as they arise. All truth is God's truth, and careful testing of new methods will lead to the truth concerning them.

In middle to upper elementary school, children have overcome these naturally-occurring learning differences which occur in the **pre-operational** stage, and it is now appropriate to teach them more advanced concepts. However, they still are most effectively taught in a **hands on** manner, using **concrete** materials (thus the reason for the name of the stage-- **Concrete_Operations)**. Manipulating bottle caps, plastic bear counters, or buttons helps the process of addition or subtraction become vivid and internalized. However, not all children reach this ability at the same time. Again, the wise teacher must, as Montessori warned, observe the child and from him learn what should be taught at the particular time. A good teacher is constantly **diagnosing and prescribing** what is appropriate to teach, both to individuals and to groups within the class. The further children advance in grade level, the <u>wider</u> will be the difference between the ability levels of the top child in the class and the slowest child in the same class. By third grade, for instance, most classrooms will contain children who would "test out" from Kindergarten to fifth grade or above. Thus, it is impossible to teach (effectively) by having all the children "on the same page of the book" at the same time. The teacher who does this (and we all know that many do) is actually "teaching to the middle," with the top students bored and the slower students frustrated.

This delicate balance of just enough challenge for the child, to keep him challenged but not frustrated, is a concept called the **problem of the match** by J. McVicker Hunt. As mentioned previously, Hunt believed that almost all learning problems, classroom discipline problems, and educational failures were due to the **match** (between the difficulty level of the material and the child's ability) being inappropriate. While I might not be willing to agree that this is the <u>only</u> thing causing educational failures, I would agree that such "mismatches" do cause major problems. Finding and keeping the right **match** for each child is one of the most difficult, but also most essential, skills of teaching. And the process will call for constant monitoring and adjusting. That's one reason that teaching never gets dull!

It's important to realize that even after the teacher diagnoses the child's ability level, the amount of challenge needed for each student will vary greatly. For the child who has had a great deal of failure, finding material where he can succeed fairly easily is essential in order to keep him from giving up and saying, "What's the use--I just can't do school work, I guess I'm just dumb or something!" On the other hand, for a child who always "knows the answer," it's important not to let him "slide by" with minimum effort. These children must come to a realization that, "What you are able to do is God's gift to you. What you do with it is your gift to God." These "gifted" children sometimes are content to be lazy, and thus need us as teachers to challenge them to get excited about learning. This can best be accomplished during the elementary school years by a combination of discovering their interests and helping them to pursue those in an advanced fashion, and by appealing to their desire to be more "grown up."

In addition to working with individual students which you know to be "gifted," always include in your group discussions a few **challenge questions** that represent knowledge or learning processes (such as research skills) that are typical of classes several years advanced from the grade level you are teaching. Then, observe carefully whether you have anyone who can respond to such **challenges**. This will be part of your **diagnosis**, and may frequently lead to the identification of a child you had not previously perceived to be "gifted."

By the time children reach these "middle elementary" years, they will have had considerable opportunity to practice the "mechanics" of **addition** and **subtraction,** and will be beginning to become acquainted with **multiplication** and **division**. No matter how much children may want or need to learn to use calculators, don't let anybody convince you that they don't need to learn the "basics" of these mechanical operations! We are indeed a technologically dependent society, but we don't want our children to grow up to be a "technologically crippled" society. One never knows when power failures, etc. might return our land to a "survival economy," and we as teachers have a responsibility to provide our children with the skills they would need to survive!

In addition to learning the basic mechanical operations of mathematics, children must learn to associate when to use them in everyday life. After all, how often do you see nice, neat addition facts on a sheet to be solved in real life ? You have to know <u>when</u> to add, <u>what</u> to subtract, and <u>how</u> to solve real life problems, or math is useless! Nevertheless, frequently you'll hear children of this age group (or even older ones) say, "I hate word problems !" The solution here is to help them set up their <u>own</u> word problems to be solved, using classroom projects (such as making lemonade for a moneymaking project) to respond to a real need. Then they can be encouraged to combine creative writing skills and mathematics by designing a class project for buying the ingredients, making a project, marketing it, and computing the profit. It has been shown that in primitive cultures where the children are (for survival purposes) taught to sell goods to help the family to make a living, they master the concept of making change and understanding profit and loss much earlier than children in this country. Thus, it cannot be emphasized enough that everyday <u>real</u> uses of math in the child's life should be brought into the classroom to make math more meaningful and vivid for learning.

One of the key processes of learning that is applicable to all subject areas is the accessing of **higher level thinking skills**. Benjamin Bloom, a key educational authority of the Twentieth Century, has put together six levels of questioning which have been closely correlated through research with the levels of thinking that exist in the classroom. The names of these six levels in order of most difficulty, along with brief descriptions of them, are listed below in bold type. Bloom's primary philosophy is that children should not just be allowed to "parrot" the material we have caused them to memorize (**knowledge**), but required to put it into their own words (**comprehension**), solve problems with it (**application**), defend it, describe what makes it up, or tell what caused it (**analysis**), create something new based upon it (**synthesis**) and critique it (**evaluation**). Math is an excellent place to put these questioning skills into practice, as we ask children to explain, apply a mathematical concept or process to solve a problem, analyze the key components of a problem, or evaluate whether or not something will work. As we get children into the habit of not settling for the lowest level of thinking, we prepare them to use more of the mental capability that God has given them, rather than just being content with "surface" thoughts and solutions. If this process is not well under way during elementary school, it will be extremely difficult for the children to get into the habit later.

"Let no man despise thy youth..." I Timothy 4:21

As young people approach puberty, there are many stresses on their lives, especially in the present day and age. They frequently feel that we as teachers are treating them as children, while they consider themselves to be young adults. Although we need to aid them in realizing that **"with rights go responsibility,"** we also need to treat them with as much dignity as possible, for this is a great need of theirs during what is, particularly physically, a very awkward age. One way to help accomplish this is to encourage them in their need to be goal-oriented toward the future when they will, indeed, be adults.

What better way could there possibly be to teach math, at this stage, than to tie it to their vocational choice ? Whether a person desires to be a physician, an engineer, a construction worker, a business person, or a homemaker, in order to be successful, the student will need math. Find out your students' vocational choices or current interests and construct word problems for a "bank" of materials to use for practice and testing. Design these problems so that they will be intriguing, to say the least. It's really lots of fun to be creative ! I remember one high school math teacher who was constantly challenging myself and others in our class to think on a higher level (now that I think of it, this was before Bloom wrote down his Taxonomy of Educational Objectives!). One particularly creative (and challenging) problem he gave us was related, of all things, to fingernail polish. He gave us the height and diameter of a nail polish bottle (from which we had to discover the total volume), the length and width of each finger nail, and the thickness of each coat of fingernail polish on the nail. We then were challenged to discover how many times a woman could paint her fingernails from a full bottle of fingernail polish ! Now that's really **analysis** and **problem solving**! And, I can tell you, he gained a lot of prestige with his students for being so creative, as well!

Not all of your students will be college bound, but for those who are, you can prepare them for the types of classes they will be taking. As a caring Christian teacher, one of the main things each of us needs to do for our students is to help them to be successful not only now, but at the next step along life's journey. They'll remember you when they can say, "The first half of the semester of algebra in college was simple--Ms./ Mr. X had already taught me so much of that! So while the rest of the students were still struggling with mastering those concepts during the second half of the semester, I was reviewing and making my previous learning more permanent, ready to go on and learn the new material successfully !"

In math as in all learning, we must prepare our students to cope with a world we will never see. For that reason, we teach them the foundational truths and skills they will need in order to understand new discoveries as they emerge. Encouraging their natural curiosity and motivating them to continue to research and learn more about the intricacies of God's world is among the most important gifts that we can give our students. They must learn that all truth is God's truth, and they must never fear to read and study further about what scientists are discovering. If these scientists are truly scientific, reporting only those things that can be directly observed, they will indeed be reporting truth that God put into this world from the beginning but that just has not been previously discovered. Students must thus be taught to seek out the validity of articles and books, checking sources and research techniques carefully in order to avoid being misled by a reporter who has some particular reason to report deceptively.

Some Christians are extremely fearful of allowing students, even in secondary school, to read scientific articles and books about controversial areas such as cloning or other types of genetic engineering. Sadly, if they prevent Christian young people from learning the truth about these areas, where will we find Christian adults to impose the moral sanctions that need to be imposed there ? If they simply come out as unalterably opposed to everything in the area without specific arguments that the secular world will respect, Christians will be dismissed as "full of sweetness and light, but not too bright," and there will be no impact for good. God has blessed many of us with excellent thinking skills, and we must never allow the world to think that "you have to be a little stupid to believe like Christians do." God doesn't want us to hide the intellectual light that He gave us under a bushel, but to let the world know that many of the best and the brightest are His followers, and that the brightest choice we ever made was to follow Him! Remember, we are to be salt and light to the world, but if we do not remain in it (but not of it), we cannot accomplish this purpose.

CHAPTER IX

Science: A Sense of Wonder About God's World

"When I consider your Heavens, the work of Your fingers, the moon and the stars which You have ordained, what is man that You are mindful of him, and the son of man that You visit him?" Psalm 8: 3-4

Many teachers seem to be afraid that science is an area that they are not able to teach. However, in a self-contained elementary or preschool classroom, it is necessary that the teacher understand the importance of including science in the curriculum. Too often, science is simply neglected because of teacher fear of being inadequate to approach the material.

Nothing could be further from the truth! Just because advanced physicists and rocket scientists speak a lingo that is incomprehensible to most "mere mortals," don't believe that children need to be approached on that level! Jerome Bruner, whose famous **"spiral curriculum"** we discussed in the previous chapter, made the amazing statement way back in the 1950's that **any subject** can be taught **in an intellectually honest manner** to any child **at any stage of development**. This was the basis of his total theory.

But how can I, with little scientific knowledge, prepare the "budding scientist"?

The nuclear physicist didn't start out knowing those intricate formulas. However, even as a preschooler he could have understood that objects can be round, square, or oval in shape. This would be the first step on Bruner's **spiral curriculum**, an intellectually honest way to present a beginning to nuclear physics which would cycle back around when he was older to lead him to shapes of atoms, orbits of electrons, and studying the nucleus of the atom. Of course, there are many stages of the spiral in between those two extremes. The fortunate thing is that those of us working with children ten years old and under do not have to understand these intricacies in order to begin the process. What we do have to understand is the necessity to hook onto the God-given sense of curiosity and excitement in learning about their world that young children demonstrate. We then present them with developmentally appropriate, "hands on" experiences that they can embrace with enthusiasm. These experiences begin the process of learning scientific concepts in such a delightful way they don't even realize they are learning!

To give an example of a classroom activity that demonstrates a basic scientific concept, let me tell you about a science fair project my daughter put together when she was in first grade (by the way, she's now a physician!). Every scientist will need to understand the concept that air expands when warmed and contracts when chilled. Later, he will understand that the distance between molecules, speed of electrons, etc. are involved. But, in preschool or first grade, just realizing how air changes when it is heated or cooled begins the understanding. To make it "hands on," our experiment involved putting rubber balloons on three coke bottles (they were glass in those days, which made them heavier and enabled the ability to stand up in water). One of the bottles was simply set on the table, one was placed into a pan of water with ice in it, and one was placed into a pan of water that was near the boiling point. It soon became apparent that the balloon over the hot water began to expand, the balloon over the ice water became shriveled as the air in the bottle contracted and pulled the air out of the balloon, and both could be compared with the balloon on the bottle which had experienced no changes in temperature.

In a classroom, after you let the children help you put together such a demonstration, ask them what happened to the three balloons. A good teacher would allow the children to make guesses at why this was happening. Give them plenty of time to think about it. Then, not belittling their answers, the teacher would say something like, "You've really come up with some good guesses at the answer–that's using your brain! But this is such a new subject for you that I'm afraid I have you stumped. Let me tell you the real reason this happened, so you can go home and tell mom and she'll know how smart you are in science! When air gets warmer, it expands, meaning it takes up more room. That's why the balloon on the bottle with the hot water began to get bigger–the air in the bottle had to have some place to go. When air is cooled, it contracts, or takes up less space. That's why the balloon on the bottle in the ice water got all shriveled up. As the air in the bottle cooled, it took up less space, so the air in the balloon was pulled into the bottle, and the balloon shriveled up. Now, which of you can tell me what happened?" Since it is a major scientific concept, over the next few days and weeks the teacher might say, "When air is heated it _____" and allow the children to shout out the correct response. (Yes, there are a <u>few</u> times to let children shout out in the classroom, and demonstrating knowledge is a good time. Celebrate the learning!)

A good time to review and have a little "drill" on such concepts is during those times when the class is lined up, perhaps waiting to go to lunch, for the dismissal bell to ring, or some other time in the schedule when they must just "wait." Such idle waiting produces what is known as "dead time," which frequently leads to misbehavior due to boredom. Therefore, take advantage of the time to have quick quizzes (make it a game by saying such things as, "Riddle-a-diddle, riddle-a-diddle! Who among you can answer my riddle?"), both in the interest of preventing misbehavior and because of good utilization of every classroom minute for learning. These times are also good for drills on math facts, finding the rhyming word that "makes sense" from a poem read by the teacher, naming an animal (food, classmate's name, etc.) that begins with a certain letter, etc. As a matter of fact, any short, important learning that will profit by skill drill should be ideal for those three- to five- minute "dead times" that can be disastrous for bringing about pushing and shoving while waiting in line. And, unlike continuing skill drill for 20 or 30 minutes, these short times will not be boring, but stimulating.

What is the " heart" of the scientific method?

The very key of the scientific method is becoming an observer of everything going on, and documenting what has been seen. This fits in perfectly with the way God has designed the child to be highly curious and exploratory of his environment. However troublesome these traits in children may sometimes be for teachers, it is important that we channel them into the right directions for learning , rather than trying to squelch them completely. God, as always, had a reason for the way He designed children. He wanted to get them to this earth ready and eager to learn!

Scientists value what can be seen and experienced, not what has been told to them by others. Thus, the scientific method is all about careful first-hand observation. But, you may say, don't we want our children to learn to live a life of faith without having to prove and experience everything? Yes, of course we do! But we don't want them to have faith in the wrong things or the wrong people, otherwise they might be seriously deceived by such scoundrels as Jim Jones who, when his false cult was about to be revealed for what it truly was, convinced his followers to drink poison. Therefore, we want to teach our children to observe and think through what they have seen in their environment. Christ has warned us, "But evil men and imposters will grow worse and worse, deceiving and being deceived." II Timothy 3:13 Likewise, we should not fear studying our world, for scripture also admonishes us, "God has not given us a spirit of fear, but of power and of love and of a sound mind."II Timothy 1:7 God has given us the sound minds to carefully examine the evidence surrounding us. And remember, as we discover what is in our environment, unswayed by human "spin," we learn that "All truth is God's truth."

In science, "primary sources" are those who have themselves witnessed something, and then give exact and accurate testimony about it. "Secondary sources" are those who put their own "spin" on what primary sources have said. Those who don't know the difference are at the mercy of radio commentators, newspapers, and yes, even books which have been falsely twisted to confuse the reader. Our children need to be taught to observe for themselves and to trust those primary sources that they know are trustworthy, such as parents, ministers, Christian teachers, and others who have proved themselves to be honorable. They also need to be taught to test all things that they hear, by the process of filtering them through scripture for validity. The scripture has not spoken extensively on each and every subject; but where it has spoken, filtering the world's teaching through scripture allows Christians to keep what is in agreement or at least does not contradict scripture, and throw away the rest. Trends will come and go, but God's truth remains forever as our guide. Isn't it wonderful to know that God and His Word are truly a still point in a changing world? And we can hold the world's theories up against His truth to determine which worldly concepts are valid.

All truth is God's truth! This is the bedrock of assurance that we need not fear true scientific endeavor. How can scientists, through true observation, come up with something untrue by observing God's creation? Real scientists will not accept a precept unless they have directly observed it. This doesn't bode well for witnessing to them, for faith, by its very nature, cannot be proved. However, statistics show that most dedicated scientists do come to a belief in God. As they observe carefully the wonders of God's creation, most of them find it impossible to believe that such intricate beauty evolved from sheer chance. Therefore, even though they have not ben able to see God directly, they come to a knowledge of Him through observing His creation and the power of their own reasoning. These steps God uses to draw them to Himself. Scripture verifies this by saying, "For since the creation of the world , His invisible attributes are clearly seen, being understood by the things that are made, even His eternal power and Godhead, so that they are without excuse." Romans 1:20

But children need guidance in their exploration.

Effective science lessons for young children involve a lot of "stage setting." Just as you might set up the coke bottles and balloons experiment for them to assemble and talk about, leading to conceptual learning, there are many other scenarios which can be used to help children "construct" their own learning. This is called the **constructivist** approach, for children are led to discover these truths for themselves, through teacher guidance and labeling. Just showing them objects or processes and giving them labels will not result in the long-term memory of learning that comes from a vivid experience of self-discovery learning. There's something about that "aha" discovery that causes events to remain vivid even in the process of recall for adults. For children, who are so much more concrete in their thinking, it is a "must" for effective learning.

Cooking is an excellent way to get across many scientific concepts. It offers opportunities for children to view how things change when they are heated or cooled. It also is a multi sensory approach involving smelling and tasting in addition to the more usual methods of seeing, hearing, and touching. Indeed, that's how a baby comes into this world ready to learn. Have you noticed that as soon as they have the coordination to do so, they will try to put everything into their mouths? That's one way they learn about their world. Although our young children have learned that putting everything into their mouths is both unsanitary and dangerous, they still have a much greater sensitivity of taste and smell than adults do. These senses gradually become less keen with age. Accordingly, experiences that involve smell and taste have special "brain markers" to link the learning with key parts of the brain for retention.

One of the beginning scientific concepts that can be easily shown to young children and and understood by them is the three states of matter (solid, liquid, and gas). Ice cubes (solid) can be placed into an electric skillet for heating, asking the children first what they think will happen when the ice is heated. Many of them will excitedly tell you that it will melt. Accept this and say, let's watch what happens. Ask them questions to keep them "with you" during the demonstration. Then tell them that you have some new scientific terms for them to go home and tell their parents about. The ice is a solid, and when it is heated it becomes a liquid. Ask them what they think will happen if you continue to heat the water. This will stump most of them, and after you've waited for it to form so they can see it, you have the opportunity to introduce the word "steam." This will probably be new to many. However, others will tell you all about how steam is used in steam engines, which you can greet with pleasure, bragging on how much they know! Point out that the steam is called a gas, and then summarize by telling them that solid, liquid, and gas are the three states of matter. Probably you will only set up the experiment once, but be sure to refer to it often, reviewing what they learned and asking them to tell you the three states of matter. Again, remind them to go home and tell their parents how they are learning to be scientists at school!

Just as a building is not constructed haphazardly, but with a plan, so **constructivist** learning must be well planned, and will need some **scaffolding** at various times, just as we discussed previously in the chapter on the teaching of reading. When putting up a building, until it has the stability to support itself, scaffolding is erected to keep it upright and safe. Later, when it is no longer needed, it is removed. The same process is a good description of the teacher's role in discovery, constructivist learning. Years ago, educational experts thought that the teacher should only prepare the environment and then step out of the picture and let the children discover it. However, in the ice/water/steam experiment, for example, the children would see change taking place, but they would have no "labels" for what was happening, nor would they understand that the solid/liquid/gas connection would be an important concept for future use. This part of the "scaffolding" must be supplied by the teacher, or the learning will not be able to be stored and categorized in the child's brain for future use.

If yours is a school that insists on worksheets to take home, wait to have a worksheet until after you have taught the concept experientially. That way, this proper use of a worksheet will aid in making the learning permanent. But do take the time to write newsletters to your parents extolling the virtues of "hands on" learning, and inviting them to visit your classroom to see the many ways of learning that you use.

Classroom plants and animals bring science to life!

Having animals in the classroom produces much learning in young children. Since most of our classrooms are predominantly made up of children from the city rather than from the agrarian societies that previously existed, many of them know very little about animals. Learning the necessities of caring for animals can be both educational and a method of building awareness of the need for responsibility.

For another example of the use of animals, growing silkworms in the classroom offers a rich opportunity to teach about the oriental cultures where silk production began as a cottage industry. History and geography naturally take their places beside the vast scientific learning from such a unit. This is an example of the making of **connections**, widely touted as a superior educational technique. When God put us into the world to learn, He didn't separate us into Social Studies classes and Science classes. The natural way to learn is integrated, pulling knowledge from all areas at once. That's the way a child learns every day of his life before coming to school (and the way we as adults learn most things, too!). Now, educational specialists are discovering that God's original way of learning is the best (although, of course, they might not identify it as God's way!). As the children watch the silkworms progress through the metamorphosis process of spinning cocoons and emerging as silk moths (Science), they can learn about the intrigue of the ancient Chinese culture that discovered how to produce silk, making it a crime punishable by death for anyone to reveal the process to other lands (Social Studies)! The fact that the silkworm eggs were originally smuggled out of the country by a princess who wed a prince from another country is pretty exciting. She actually hid the silkworm eggs in the folds of her wedding turban! For additional information, I recommend two books: *Silkworms and Science: The Story of Silk* by Elizabeth K. Cooper and *Silkworms* by Sylvia A. Johnson. The first book is no longer in print, but many libraries still have a copy. It is excellent for building an overall background for a silkworm project. The second book has beautiful illustrations. Finally, there is much information now available on the Internet about caring for silkworms in the classrooms.

Plant projects also can yield much "hands on" learning. A simple but interesting project is to get some lima beans and place them between dampened paper towels and the outside of a glass jar. If you can get enough baby food jars or other small jars, it is helpful to let each child have his own jar to place in the window and check daily for signs of growth. As the roots and upper sprouts emerge, you can talk with the children about the parts of plants that are necessary for survival and why they are necessary. Another interesting thing to do with plants is to take small plants (perhaps the result of the lima bean sprouting) and put some in the dark, some in the bright window sill, and some in a less-well-lighted part of the classroom. Then, let the children talk about the differences and come up with the reasons that some did better than others. Also, you can take a plant that is watered every day, one that is not watered at all, and one that is watered only when the soil shows it is needed, and talk about those results. See how easy it is? Just use your own ideas of things to try out with plants, and let children make discoveries that lead to scientific concepts that will be learned in a vivid manner they will seldom forget.

During the time when I taught in a church-related preschool, the kindergarten classes called the Science Center the "Worship Center." I found that strange at first, but then I realized that having an appreciation for the beauties of God's creation by viewing plants, animals, seashells, rocks, etc. was indeed an activity that causes thankfulness and worship of God as Creator. In like fashion, showing reverence for this created beauty should result in a desire to conserve and protect God's perfect gifts. Through an enthusiastic introduction to observing and appreciating the world God has given us, we instill in the child a sense of responsibility for respecting and preserving all forms of life. This can even tie in with a unit on the damage done by littering. That responsibility for caring for the world was ever so, as evidenced from the scripture, which says, "Then the Lord God took the man and put him in the garden of Eden to tend and keep it."
Gen. 2:15

All truth is God's truth!

An underlying fear among Christian teachers of approaching science lies in the fallacious belief that science and faith contradict each other. As Paul would way, "May it never be!" As previously stated, the true scientist believes only what can be clearly demonstrated and observed about the world . Thus, he can only demonstrate and observe the laws which God has put into place in His creation. As a teachers of science, we are teaching children to pay close attention to what is happening around them—a good practice for many reasons, even physical safety. As they learn the fundamental truths of observing God's creation, they will be able to refute those false notions that have been "tacked on" to science by "pseudo-scientists." When they speak to us of evolution, our children will be able to ask what observable proof they have of evolution (there is none). They can, of course, point to signs that animal life has changed through the years, but this is simply an example of how God has created animals to change so that they can survive when their environment changes. There is absolutely no proof that man has evolved in the way that "pseudo-scientists" suggest. In fact, for your children most interested in this issue, make them aware that there is a huge documentation of evidence called "Creation Science" which has great documentation that life began as the Bible indicates. Nevertheless, belief still comes to placing faith in the Bible, for God never intended for us to be able to prove everything. "Without faith it is impossible to please God." Heb. 11:6 He created us to depend on Him, believe what He has told us in His scriptures, and obey Him. Through our faith in Him, we glorify His name in all the world!

CHAPTER X

Social Studies:
How the Child Relates to His World

"Let each of you look out not only for his own interests, but also for the interests of others." Phil. 2:4

But, what about ME! says the child.

One of the most difficult things we face as parents and teachers of the very young, is the fact that the infant comes into this world concerned only with having his own needs gratified. He wants what he wants when he wants it! Ask any young parent who has been aroused for that middle of the night feeding by a baby screaming so loudly that you would think that he himself was being devoured, rather than he was only hungry! Perhaps God formed the infant this way so that, for survival, there would be no doubt that he needed to be fed, comforted, or rescued from danger. We know that there was a reason for this self-centeredness. However, as the child grows older, being centered on self continues until we patiently work to teach him to wait, share, and otherwise accommodate the needs of others. This is necessary in order for him to fit into life in a way that will be acceptable to those around him.

We all have known adults who are still so centered on their own needs that they cannot seem to take into account the needs of others. These adults are truly their own worst enemies, driving away the very people who could provide them with the companionship, help, and love they need. Nobody likes to be around people who are centered only upon meeting their own needs. So, how do we help the child move from that position to one in which he begins to take into consideration the needs of those around him? That falls into the area of Social Studies, which, by definition, is how man relates to himself, others, and the physical world around him.

To begin with, meet them where they are!

Educational research suggests that children go through developmental stages that will give us a clue for this teaching to be most effective. Since the very young child is predominantly self-centered by nature, the first lessons should be centered around him and how he relates to his closest environment: his family. Brothers, sisters, mothers, fathers, and family routines are our first opportunity to build empathy in the child. Empathy is partially defined as "experiencing the feelings of another person."Empathy is based on the emotions, not cognition, and since research suggests the child's brain may not comprehend the same way as an older child or an adult, emotions are the best route to early learning. Piaget had originally proposed that a child under the age of seven years was unable to think about another person's needs. He was working strictly on a cognitive theory. But later research has shown that children will show signs of distress about others' pain at a much earlier age, especially when it involves someone they have come to love. This ability comes not from cognition, but from emotional experience, or "feelings.".

A classic study concerning the inborn ability to sense and respond to another person's distress was conducted by a man named Martin Hoffman. He conducted a classic study in newborn nurseries to examine the likelihood of babies waking and crying when they heard other infants crying. Of course, you say, newborns are disturbed by any noise. That is what most people believed, but Hoffman was convinced that there was something else involved, and he set out to test whether or not this was the case. He went into a newborn nursery where there were a lot of infants crying, made a tape of this, then scientifically analyzed the tape for pitch, loudness, and spacing of both variables. He then designed a tape of neutral sounds that were varying in exactly the same pitches and to the same degree of loudness in sequence. Next, he took both the tape of neutral sounds and the tape of babies crying into large numbers of newborn nurseries and played them individually. He wanted to determine whether babies would awake and cry equally when each tape was played. As he had suspected, significantly higher numbers of babies awakened and began to cry when the tape was played of actual babies crying. From this, along with other studies he conducted, he stated that babies arrive at birth with an inborn natural tendency to respond to others who are in pain.

Isn't it beautiful to know that God starts us off on the track of being distressed when someone around us is distressed? It is only through our simultaneous tendency to be self-centered that we sometimes choose to grow away from this pattern. This tendency to feel the pain of others has been called **empathy**, and it is very important in the moral development of the child. It differs from sympathy in that sympathy can border on pity, which is not usually as helpful to those who are suffering as truly understanding why they are suffering and wanting to do something to help. **Empathy** involves feeling pain unless we are able to help that other person. That is why the newborns cried more in the nurseries when they heard other babies crying than when they simply heard noises that awakened them. They sensed the suffering of another baby like themselves, and the only way they knew to help was their God-given ability to cry and "call for Mommy to come help."

As stated previously, Piaget thought that children were totally self-centered and unable to understand another person's point of view until they were around seven years old. But Piaget's theory was cognitive, not emotional. What he didn't understand, and Hoffman later added to the picture, was that infants' and toddlers' emotions are much more highly developed than their cognitive abilities. After proving that newborns showed signs of distress when they heard other babies in distress, Hoffman made further studies of toddlers. These are situations that you may have seen for yourself if you are around young children. Toddlers would seek to comfort those around them, but their method of comfort was not cognitively appropriate (remember what Piaget said about their thinking skills). You may have seen a child begin to cry if he sees his mother crying, or you may have even seen him go and offer his pacifier to his mother in order to try to comfort her. Young preschoolers, when they see their friend fall and hurt himself, may run to get their own mother to help him, even though the injured child's mother might be right there! You see, the small child cannot imagine that anyone would want something different from what he would want in the same situation (pacifier, his own mother, etc.) But the point is, a very young child already has this sense of **empathy,** which can be defined as an ability to share in another person's emotions or feelings. We'll return to this concept in more depth when we discuss moral development, which is placed in the category of social studies by the academic world. But for now, the important thing to remember is that knowing a child's developmental characteristics at the earliest age will enable us to encourage his better tendencies and teach him more effectively.

Work from the inside of the child's world, out!

Social studies instruction, then, begins with the first group interaction that surrounds the child—his own family. Textbooks define social studies as, "the study of how a person relates to himself, other people, and the physical world around him." Think about how that relates to a child and his family. This is where we begin.

As the child begins to venture out into other groups, such as his church family, his preschool classes, etc., these become the next focus of social studies. Although we continue to talk about getting along well with our families, gradually those boundaries expand to include other groups familiar to the child. The first learning about rules naturally occurs in all these settings. People have to have rules and be willing to work together and help each other in order for any form of government to be successful. Unless this is understood at an early age, conceiving of an effective government will be much more difficult later on in life.

From the protective, encouraging world of family, church, and preschool classroom, the child emerges into what one textbook writer calls the "jungle" of school-age peer relationships and competition of the elementary classroom. It is in this setting that he may be exposed to the concept of being a leader as having responsibility to help those he leads, and of being a follower as having responsibility to follow the rules set up for the group. Every child needs experiences in both roles, for as adults we all need to know how to function effectively in both capacities. First experiences with government may be encountered through voting to elect class officers who have defined responsibilities for the benefit of the class. Elections are difficult for the child, because where there are winners, there must also be losers. However, it is through this process that the child learns from experience about the democratic process. It is vital to communicate that each child plays an important role in the class, even though he may not be elected to "top office." Up until about grade three, it is probably better for each child to have an assigned role of specific responsibilities in the class, because the competitive process of an election may have more damaging effects than educative ones. Beginning in third grade, class elections may be carefully attempted, but with much caution and explanation by the teacher regarding the importance of each member of the class as a part of the "team.".

The child soon becomes aware that he lives in a neighborhood, and that the neighborhood contains his home, church, and school. He therefore begins to understand, in ever-increasing circles, how the world exists outside himself. Learning the name of the city or town where he resides is the next step, and he soon should be led to realize the many things around him that are located in this city or town, such as parks, libraries, grocery stores, etc. After he understands fully the concept of his neighborhood (or community) being part of the city, and learns the city's name, the next step is to identify the state in which he lives. Again, he will need to understand that the state is large enough to contain many cities and towns. At this time, usually in fourth or fifth grade, beginning introduction to such things as the governor, the state legislature, and the state mascot and flower should occur. It is very common for young children to confuse their city name with their state name, and there is a need to constantly teach and reteach the concepts of city and state. As familiar as this information is to us, it is hard to realize that it is totally new to young children. That being the case, it is wise to remember that research says most people need to encounter new information something like twenty times before it becomes permanent in their minds. If a child has a learning disability or is ill or otherwise distracted when information is presented, it may easily be many more times than that! Sharing this information should keep you from being discouraged when you spent most of the previous day emphasizing that our city's name as Dallas, and Johnny comes in the next day announcing, "Texas" when asked the name of his city!

Mapping—using visual images

As children begin to understand how maps show locations and their relationships to one another (a subject about which, unfortunately, there is some disagreement concerning whether they are understood by young children), simple maps may be drawn of their classroom or their home as related to their school. Such first maps are the most understandable ones to the child at an early age.

Beginning with simple maps of locations familiar to the child, such concepts as north, south, east, and west on a map may be easily established. Set up the classroom to represent a map. Then ask designated children to play the game of going to the north on the map (the front of the room), the east of the map (the right side of the room) etc. As they become actively involved in experiencing the four locations on the map (and have fun because they are playing a game!), you can soon have them draw a map of the room, with north, south, east, and west marked (For simplification of the map-teaching process, it is best to designate the front of the room as north, even though it probably is not true north on the compass.). They can then draw in the teacher's desk, classroom desks, etc. Don't proceed too rapidly through these steps, however. Be sure the directionality is understood from "acting it out (moving to the positions) before trying to have them draw it represented in a map. Again, these concepts may seem very simple to us, but new information to the children will take many exposures to be effective. (At least twenty to be permanent—remember?) If drawing a representation is introduced before the concept is really understood, they may be able to "parrot" a correct response, but the information will not transfer to other maps and will thus be useless. Spending a short amount of time each day "playing the game" for about a week will give the children active time to recall what they have learned on the previous day and will provide for the children who are absent when this is first introduced. But, from the very first, "talk it up" as being an introduction to "what some adults even find difficult—reading a map!" Children love to be able to go home and brag to their parents that they are learning something that their teacher said was really hard, but that they are smart enough to learn!

After children have learned to draw simple maps representing their known environment, the step they are frequently asked to do, very early in most curriculum, is to color or draw a map of their own state. The more "hands on" this activity can be, the better it will be for true comprehension and retention. One way to make it more vivid than just a coloring sheet is to mimeograph state outlines for each child and have them to fill them in with home-made play dough (which can also be a math lesson in measuring and preparing) and put in a marker of some kind representing their own city. Various depths of play dough may also be used to contrast elevations in those states which have mountainous regions.

When the child's city and state are thoroughly learned, he is ready to look in depth at the United States and to be shown about the many states which all fit together to form a map of the United States of America. This doesn't mean, however, that he will never have encountered that concept before. Just as we surround a child with print before he is ready to learn to read, and he picks up some awareness just from encountering it, so a child may have worked with a giant puzzle of the United States of America long before he is truly cognizant of what cities, states, and countries actually are. God designs the child's mind to make sense out of his world in just this way. His brain encounters, organizes, and retains whatever is appropriate from his surroundings. The rest is discarded until a later date. These beginning concepts, then, form a type of open meshwork and organization of early experiences that "reach out and catch" new information later, when the child is ready to comprehend it. (Remember Bruner's Spiral Curriculum?)

A special teaching technique: EPRT

It may surprise you how much some children have already figured out about things, just as it may also surprise you to discover how the very most basic of concepts sometimes may not have been discovered at all. One of the key strengths of a good teacher is to be constantly analyzing what is understood, what is not understood, and when to move on to new learning while continuing individual instruction for children who need it. It's kind of like a constant "testing," not through pencil and paper, but through informally questioning the children and observing them. Much of this is accomplished through walking around the classroom and observing the students while they work independently (a good teacher spends very little time behind her desk!). However, there is a technique that can yield much information from group settings. It is called EPRT, or Every Pupil Response Technique, and is a great time-saver in figuring out whether or not some specific learning has been accomplished, and by which students. It's important to work rather quickly in using this technique, or otherwise the "classroom smarties" will be looking around and making fun of those who get the wrong answer. For the same reason, establish an "eyes to the front of the classroom" rule, especially for older children. One example of this technique is to ask true or false questions, telling the children that "thumbs up" means "true," "thumbs down" means "false," and "thumbs to the side" means "I don't know." The class should be assured that there will be questions for which they aren't supposed to know the answers , so nobody should be ashamed of saying they don't know.

Once you understand the EPRT technique, you should be able to design many ways of assessing various concepts. For example, when preschoolers are learning their colors, have them sit with a box of crayolas in front of each one. Then say, "Everybody hold your red crayon over your head," etc. It is easy to see which ones have to look around to see what the others are doing before holding up their crayon. Later, you might want children to know, in phonics instruction, what is the first letter in a certain word you call out for them. If you invest in a classroom-sized number of small slates, each child can write the answer on his slate, then hold it in front off his chest so that you can see it, but others have to "crane their neck" to do so. These little slates will enable you to practice the EPRT technique in almost any subject. The more you use it, the more you will appreciate this "bird's-eye-view" of what you have actually taught and how much has been received. At first, it may be discouraging to learn that much re-teaching is necessary. But remember, research says if they haven't encountered the material somewhere else, it may take twenty times of repeating before they actually "get it."

Finding our places in God's world

Moving out from our nation, the Social Studies next will focus on the world and how our nation relates to it. Much international teaching can flow from "the teachable moment," which should be utilized at all teaching levels as a natural motivator and capturing of the child's inquisitive nature. If your church or school has a country which they specifically sponsor through missions, this is a natural place to start a brief overview of the world. It is always advisable to have a globe in the classroom so that the children will, from the very start, see how all the countries fit together. The globe also helps in science instruction, showing how the sun seems to rise and fall each day, but that the phenomenon is really caused by the earth's rotation. Since the globe has a very small representation of each country, it is next appropriate to move from showing the children the United States and the country of study on the globe, to a map of the country for greater detail.

As children become aware of the globe and the many countries that are represented on it, they will begin to have a grasp of how our country fits into the overall world situation and relates to other countries. They should also be made aware of our responsibility both to appreciate the world that God has made and to protect its environment and the people in other countries that are also His creation.

Your classroom or school may subscribe to a weekly newspaper written with appropriate news events reported at different levels for specific grades of children. Any major news event gives a golden opportunity to show the location on the globe and maps. Additionally, this should be enlarged by talking about and showing pictures and/or objects from the people of other lands. Short stories, either fictional or factual, about the cultures of other lands will be an excellent example of "connections" across the curriculum between reading and social studies. These may be read aloud by the teacher or by the children themselves if the reading level is not too difficult. And, by the way, students never grow too old to enjoy hearing a good story read aloud by a good reader. My first teaching position was in eighth grade, and the class quietened during my "read-aloud time" in a way that happened at no other time during the day! My disciplinary skills were not well developed when I started out, but I dearly loved reading and somehow was able to communicate that to my class. Although I didn't know it then, this was a great example of the truism that "Enthusiasm is caught, not taught."

As you make the foreign cultures more "real" to your students, it is natural to emphasize the differences. However, they should come to realize that we are more alike than different, since all of us have a need to be safe, loved, fed, and clothed. And, of course, all of us need to learn about God's love for us, and how He sent His Son to prove that love. These likenesses and differences can be particularly important when children come to realize that many children around the world do not have what children in the United States take for granted, such as running water, enough food to eat, clothes to wear, or a school to attend. A spirit of thankfulness for the blessings of living in our country needs to be instilled in children at an early age. Additionally, they should come to realize that we have been "blessed to be a blessing," and that our abundance should be shared by helping others. This spirit of thankfulness will not only help them to want to reach out to others, but will also protect them from a major epidemic that plagues our culture currently. Although we are, without a doubt, the wealthiest of countries, strangely enough this epidemic that threatens our children is depression. This "epidemic," (which can be called that because of the large numbers afflicted by it, many of whom commit suicide, get heavily hooked on drugs, or commit random acts of violence) is a tendency, from the earliest years, toward depression. Although there are many causes for the rise of depression in this country, one simple thing that we as teachers can do to help stem the tides is to constantly show the children how much we all have to be thankful for. Research has shown that a spirit of depression and a spirit of thankfulness cannot co-exist!

Wow! What an opportunity (and responsibility) we have as teachers! This teaching should not be done in a "preachy" or guilt-inducing manner, however, for that will be rejected. It should be demonstrated by the teacher, first of all. After reading a story of another land which emphasizes their needs, she might say, "My, I never realized how thankful I should be to have so much food available to me and never have to worry about going to bed hungry!" Or, she could come into class one morning and say, "Boys and girls, I am so glad we can be here together. In (insert specific country), I understand that there are very few schools or teachers, and the children cannot always come to school because it is so far and there is no way to get to a school. Also, they have to stay home all day and work at weeding the crops or carrying what little water there is, so that their family will have food. And when they can go to school, the teachers don't have beautiful books or maps. They just have to teach the best they can without them. How blessed we are!" Then, if it is a Christian school, this is a good time to just stop and have prayers of thanksgiving. The teacher could demonstrate, then invite the children to give sentence prayers about specifics things for which they are thankful.

Although we will emphasize how people from other cultures are different from us, it is also very important to emphasize that they are more like us than different from us. They all want to have friends. They all want to have a chance to learn and grow. They all want a chance to be successful. Again, if this is a Christian school, emphasis can be given that Christ died for these people, just as He died for us, but some of these children have never heard about this. This emphasis on the needs of others around the world and our responsibilities to be concerned about helping to meet those needs, leads naturally into a discussion of the child's moral development. As Christians, this should be extremely important to us. The secular world categorizes moral development under the umbrella of Social Studies. This is easier to understand when we return to our earlier definition of Social Studies, "the study of how a person relates to himself, other people, and the physical world around him." Moral development is encapsulated in whether a person feels his own needs are predominant over everything else (how he relates to himself), whether he sees other people as partners in life's journey or merely stepping stones to help him get ahead (how he relates to other people), and whether the physical world around him is to be greedily exploited for his own use or protected for the use of others and future generations (how he relates to the physical world around him).

"Now the purpose of the commandment is love from a pure heart, from a good conscience, and from sincere faith." I Timothy 1:5

One of the descriptions that secularists have given for moral development is "teaching a child to be honest, kind, and just." That seems like it could tie in very nicely with the scripture given above. If a person is truly honest, kind, and just, he would certain ly be showing a pure heart and a good conscience. And as Christians we know that without sincere faith in Jesus Christ we would be unable to have either a pure heart or a good conscience! The sin nature causes us to constantly have to turn back to Christ for cleansing and forgiveness so that our heart can become pure again and our conscience restored.

It is important as teachers that we set a good example for the children to follow morally as well as intellectually, yet we must not lead them to believe that we are perfect. If you try to make children believe that you always have all the answers and always do the right thing, sooner or later they will find out otherwise and stop trusting you at all. When you don't know the answer to a question, never say, "Johnny, I'd like you to look that up tonight and report about it to class tomorrow." (Can you believe that some teachers have actually done just this?!) Instead, say something like this, "Johnny, that is a good question, and I don't have the answer for you right now. But I'll do some study tonight and try to tell you the answer tomorrow." When tomorrow comes, be sure to comment on the need to answer Johnny's question (be careful–it's so easy to get busy and forget!). In addition, tell where you looked for the answer (discussing use of the internet , encyclopedias, history books, or whatever sources are pertinent) and what you found. Thus you are teaching the children how you as a teacher search for answers to questions, as well as showing that it is no disgrace to not have all the answers!

That scenario of not having all the answers may be humbling enough, but how much more humbling it is to realize that you judged harshly or with incomplete evidence against a child. Or, perhaps you made a wrong decision about punishing the whole class for something that really was caused by only one or a few individuals. Many teachers feel that if they admit to the children that they have made a mistake, they will lose their respect. Actually, students come to greatly respect a teacher who is willing to admit that she made a mistake and to ask for forgiveness! The teacher might say something like this, "Boys and girls, I want you to know that after I went home last night and thought it over I realized that I made a mistake when I _____ because _____. I would like to ask you to forgive me. I will try to be more careful in the future." Then, if a punishment handed down needs to be changed, change it. Again, we are modeling for the children that 1)everyone (even the teacher) makes mistakes (so it isn't the end of the world when they make one), and 2) if you make a mistake, it is important to acknowledge that mistake and ask for forgiveness.

Earlier in this chapter, we discussed the development of the altruism that is present within the newborn baby. Since this is a God-given characteristic which our Creator has established within the youngest of infants, it would seem that it would need no special encouragement for it to develop. But, we all know that Satan is ever at work trying to offset God's perfect purposes. Since Satan knows that his time is limited before Christ returns and casts him into the lake of fire, he seems to be working overtime to offset good things with bad, particularly in the lives of the very young. It is during these early years that children are most impressionable, and Satan knows if he can leave his imprint early, it will be more difficult to eradicate later when the personality is formed and literally begins to "harden," or become permanent. But, "We are not ignorant of his devices," (II Cor. 2:11). Therefore, we know how important it is to mold the child for good during those impressionable early years.

As we try to capitalize on these early beginnings of **altruism**, the ability to feel pain when someone else is in pain and to desire earnestly to relieve that pain, there are several things that scientific studies have proven are effective in aiding this development. Remember, true science only sets out to observe what happens and document it. True science, therefore, searches for truth, although some scientists will try to put their own "spin" on theories that cannot be proved, such as evolution. When this happens, they are not applying the true **scientific method**, which requires only observing and recording what can be seen. When scientists utilize the true **scientific method**, they are observing and recording truth. Since all truth is God's truth, there is no fear of honoring the facts derived from the true scientific method.

One of the major things that can be done in helping children to develop caring for other people in need is a classic example of how so much learning is "caught, and not directly taught." It has proven to be highly effective for the young preschool child (also for older children) to be in the company of an adult whom they respect and/or love while that adult is helping someone in need and clearly enjoying doing so. It doesn't have the same effect at all if the child hears you muttering to yourself, "Why did I agree to do this? I really don't have time for it!"

I experienced this phenomenon before the research came out concerning it, and later when I read the research, I was gratified that the Lord had led me to do the right thing to influence my younger daughter. During the time when Laura was about four years old, I used to pick up hot meals from a distribution point and deliver them to elderly shut-ins who were unable to cook for themselves but still capable of staying in their own homes. It was a program still in existence that you may have heard about called "Meals on Wheels." We also prepared at our home a small sack lunch for each recipient for the other meal of the day, since most of them were able to pour cereal into a bowl and add milk for their breakfast. I remember saying to Laura as we would go around to the houses or when we were preparing the sack lunches, "Doesn't it make you feel good to be able to help these sweet people? Many of them don't see anyone but us all day, and I think they appreciate visiting with us briefly as much as they enjoy the food." Laura took great pride in carrying part of the food as we went up the walk to each house. As an adult, she chose to be a school counselor, and has even invited teenagers who had been kicked out by their parents to live in her home! Indeed, I sometimes worried about her safety in doing such things, but it was certain that her sense of empathy was well developed!

Empathy is closely related to a phenomenon called **prosocial behavior**. Prosocial behavior is roughly defined as doing good things for other people without any ulterior motive of receiving personal reward or gain. Scientific studies have shown that this develops primarily through a process known as **induction.** Induction, as a moral development technique, consists of talking about the effects of a child's actions, whether good or bad, and helping the child to understand how he would feel when receiving this action from another. Although there is some "telling" involved, this technique is most effective when questions lead the child to tell how he would feel if someone did this to him. It is also a trait that is "more caught than taught," developing primarily by following after a respected role model. This can be an awesome responsibility for parents and teachers of the very young.

Induction and modeling after the parent or teacher are both more likely to be effective if a blend of two elements is present in the authority figure. Research has shown that both of these elements are necessary if a child is to want to be like the adult role model. The elements are **warmth** and **power**. If an adult does not seem warm and loving toward the child, there is very little likelihood that the child will pattern after the adult or absorb the adult's induction. However, it is also true that the child must respect the adult in order for this to effectively take place. This means that the adult must have firm rules (although reasonable in content and number for the age of the child) and consistently enforce them.

Sadly, many conscientious Christian parents wonder why their children do not follow their training when they are older. It usually boils down to a lack of one or the other of the two key elements. If there is little warmth or love shown but plenty of control, the child will obey through fear, but may later break away and try to live a totally different life style. However, the reason sometimes godly, warm, and loving parents who set beautiful examples may have irresponsible children is because the lack of firmness leads to over-indulgence of the children. Feeling that this "softness" demonstrates weakness, the children perceive these parents or teachers as weak rather than powerful. Ultimately, research shows that they lose respect and may go off to "do their own thing," thinking they will be powerful and find their own way. Scripture has many admonitions for the parent to prove he is "in control" at an early age. For instance, Proverbs 13:24 says,"He who spares his rod hates his son, but he who loves him disciplines him promptly." This has been interpreted by some to say that although parents may think their motive is love, actually they are not acting in the child's best interests when they allow him to continue bad behavior, for it will become an accepted habit pattern. God compares His love for us as children with the love a parent or teacher should have for a child by saying, ""For whom the Lord loves He corrects, Just as a father the son in whom he delights." Prov. 3:12

Role playing is an example of another teaching technique to encourage children to think of others' feelings and needs, rather than only of their own. The children enact a role in a situation that takes on another child's perspective while another child takes on a role with their perspective . This is particularly useful when two children feel they have been hurt by each other, yet neither can perceive that the other child has also been hurt. It can be a valuable tool in getting the children out of their ego-centrism. This activity for older children has even been shown to reduce the repetition of delinquent children's crimes. As they switch roles from their usual position, they learn the art of what psychologists call "perspective taking." Perhaps you have read the book or seen a film called "Freaky Friday" in which one day a little girl woke up and was her mother, while her mother became the little girl. It caused a lot of laughs, of course, but it was obvious that both parties learned a great deal from the transaction,

Role playing and induction both represent a blending of the cognitive and affective (feeling) learning modalities. As previously stated, children's emotions develop much earlier than their cognitive awareness, but the two can work together to aid children in their moral development. In the earliest years they learn primarily by emotions. However, just as we surround a child with simple print long before he is truly ready to read, we also offer simple cognitive explanations of moral situations along with modeling and other affective (emotion-based) techniques. This way, as soon as the child is able to understand and use reasoning, the words will be there for him. More and more we are learning that adults have traditionally tended to underestimate what the youngest children are capable of understanding.

Another concept in moral development that children may not be able to understand until about the time they approach the third grade (some earlier, some later), is the concept of **equality versus equity**. About that time, frequently it is heard in the classroom or on the playground, "It's not fair!" Children become almost obsessed with "fairness," but this is all part of their moral development the way God planned it. Parents observe from the first that if they divide something between two children, both children will think the other one got the biggest piece! The best technique there is to let one child divide it, telling him that his sibling will get first choice. You can imagine how careful the "divider" will be to see that the halves are indeed equal! But, as the children grow a little older, they must be led to understand that "equal" is not always "fair." For instance, a child who is unwell or handicapped may need a "head start" in a race. Likewise, a younger child may not have as many difficult chores as an older child, yet the younger child is not allowed to stay up as late at night as the older child. These comparisons are **equity**, which has been defined as something that is fair and just, although not exactly even. Often, complete equality is not fair and just, as the above examples have shown.

Many people question the use of rewards or punishment in establishing good moral habit patterns. Research is mixed in this area, but one thing is certain—if rewards are used, they should only be used to help get the habit started, and should not be overused to the extent that the child develops the attitude of "What will you give me if I do that?" Focus should not be on the reward, but rather on the fact that it is only a reminder to the children of what they should do anyway. Charles Spurgeon said that as a young child he was given small amounts of money for every Bible verse he memorized and for every rat he killed. As an adult, he commented that the Bible verses had been much more valuable in the long run! So, rewards and punishments should be used sparingly as an encouragement to the development of good habit patterns. These techniques should be accompanied by **induction** to emphasize the true value for one's later life of developing good habits. However, research has been fairly consistent in indicating that rewards do **not** lead children to be more altruistic. This is better accomplished by the previously described techniques of **modeling, role-playing, and induction.**

Another area of moral development that needs to be considered is called **resistance to temptation**. This the area concerning which I did my dissertation, so I'm going to have to be sure I don't put an unbalanced amount of material into this book about my area of much research. To encapsulate much of the overall findings in this area, children show a much stronger resistance to temptation (particularly when they must decide in a hurry what to do) if they have developed a strong conscience in early childhood. This occurs primarily in the "feeling" rather than "thinking" experiences of young childhood when they feel horror at things for which their bonded adults expressed horror, therefore internalizing guilt concerning those things. Sadly, some children therefore are unwittingly "programmed" to feel that being messy is very wrong (if their loved adults over-react to a spill on the carpet). Conversely, when a parent or teacher lets cruelty to another child pass with only a mild reprimand (or even ignoring the act completely), there may be no conscience development in this area. The clue for adults who would influence preschoolers for good conscience development is to allow themselves to show real distress when the child hurts another child, but give a low-key statement about being more careful when accidental spills occur.

The development of conscience does result in guilt, and here it is imperative to mention the caution of not overdoing it. While the modern world may not think guilt should ever be induced and all things should be "OK," we as Christians know that this is not true. God designed us to feel guilt so that we would refrain from doing things that we should not. Guilt is an effective controller of behavior. On the other hand, too much bringing forth of guilt can result in a psychologically damaged child who feels guilty about everything. This is known as **false guilt**. Parents are often so afraid of this that they avoid the use of conscience formation completely (except in the case of their own concern about the carpet, which they don't realize evokes guilt in the child!) They pass up the opportunity to make the child feel ashamed of having hurt the other child because they are afraid of causing guilt at all. Guilt can be compared to a sharp scalpel used in surgery. In the hands of a skilled physician it can bring great improvement in health, but used recklessly it can cause much damage. Just remember to save guilt for the really important issues, and even then to emphasize restoration through repentance and changing the conduct in the future, rather than "gunny sacking the guilt" to bring out on future occasions.

One of the most effective methods for healthy conscience development is known as **love-oriented discipline.** These techniques from research underscore what was mentioned previously about the need for a balance between **warmth** and **power**. Love-oriented discipline is based upon a warm, loving relationship between parent and child. The child must feel secure in the belief that his parents love him, regardless of behavior or misbehavior. If this dimension is missing, love-oriented techniques are ineffective. Basically, this technique involves talking to the child very seriously (and in private) after the offensive act occurs. The expression of sadness, along with disappointment in the child that he would act this way, is the key. Our Lord Jesus Christ demonstrated this type of relationship with His followers when He wept over Jerusalem, saying, "O Jerusalem, Jerusalem, the one who kills the prophets and stones those who are sent to her! How often I wanted to gather your children together, as a hen gathers her brood under her wings, but you were not willing!" Luke 13:34 If punishment must ensue, as was the case for Jerusalem, His role model tells us to enforce it with a sense of sadness, not with an "I gotcha" attitude (so easy for us to do through exasperation and acting out of the flesh).

Something that fits in well with this technique is the **attribution of good intentions**. Instead of saying, "You always treat other children harshly instead of considerately—don't you even care about other people's feelings?" say something like, "I'm sure you wouldn't have told Sarah that she was fat if you had stopped to think how that would make her feel." This causes the child to think of himself as basically a well-intentioned person who sometimes slips up in behavior, rather than developing a self-image of being a "bad" person. This self image, research tells us, will lead to the child living up to that image, whether it is negative or positive. And remember, never be afraid of valid research, for it is only reporting behavioral evidence of the truth, and all truth is God's truth. Just beware of believing what may be some researcher's interpretation of findings, or secondary sources who report only the findings that fit their agenda. It is always best to seek out the primary sources of research or to be able to have reason for confidence in the person who is a secondary source.

Another useful method for addressing both the "thinking" and the "feeling" elements of morality in the child is called **induction**. This is an example of more "talking about" situations, rather than just letting them go without consequence or punishing the child with no further comment. Again, these discussions should follow the offense as soon as it is practical to do so in privacy with the child, and at a time when there is no need to be rushed. Sometimes telling a child, "We need to talk about this later," will alert him to the fact that the behavior is serious and may have serious consequences. In truth, you may want to wait to spell out the punishment until later, which can be a punishment in itself as the child imagines how serious the punishment may be! But, the primary reason for waiting until later is so that **inductive** techniques can be used.

The first technique of induction is pointing out the consequences of the behavior to others, both those observed and possible future consequences that the child might not have considered. Some people use the "What if everyone did this?" technique if it is appropriate. This is most appropriate for such offenses as senseless littering or failure to pick up after oneself. For a hurtful offense against an individual, it is more appropriate to speak in terms of how that person must have felt. In an instance with a younger child who has not experienced a similar situation, he may have difficulty in understanding how the other child feels. In such an instance, you might say, "Do you remember how you felt when Johnny jerked the leg off your favorite doll? That is how Mary is feeling now because of what you did."

A second example of induction is to make it clear why you are establishing a rule. Rather than the old, "Because I say so!" that many of us came to resent as children, it is important that our children realize that the rules we make are for their own benefit. And, if that is true, why not tell them about that benefit? " I know you'd like to stay up later, but it's important for your health that you get enough sleep. I love you too much to let you do something that will cause you to be sick now or to not grow up to be strong and healthy." However, if the child begins to argue that he is never sick, or any other argument, it is then time to say a modified version of the old "Because I say so." More diplomatically phrased, it is, "I'm sorry you don't agree with what I know is best, but I am the adult, while you are still a child. I have a responsibility before God, who gave you to me, to use my better judgment to protect you until you are an adult yourself." This is good to remember in any situation where explanations are being made to a child concerning the use of rules or punishments. Reasoning should never be allowed to turn into arguing, and it is up to the adult to firmly draw the line here. (Remember, **power** is important, as well as **warmth**, in order to produce the desired effect.)

Finally, inductive discipline does still involve the stimulation of a reasonable amount of guilt. As the child examines the consequences of his behavior, if he is to sincerely repent of this behavior he will experience at least some guilt. Induction is a part of **love oriented** discipline. If the child does not love and respect his parents, he will not be interested in hearing their reasons for rules or their reminders of victim-related consequences.

I'd like to tell you about a little scenario I witnessed when I was supervising student teachers in kindergarten a number of years ago. The kindergarten teacher was greatly loved by her students. As a matter of fact, after school was out she frequently would receive visits from some of her former students who were all the way up into fifth grade. They would come by for a hug and a word of encouragement, as they knew they would always find that in Mrs. H. The scenario I want to share involved a child who had committed some minor offense. (I don't remember the exact offense.) Mrs. H waited until the other children were busy in their kindergarten centers, then called the offending student to herself. She got down on the child's level, put her arm around him, and drew him close to her. Then she said, sadly, "Johnny, I can't believe that you did _____;that isn't like you at all," (working on a positive, not a negative, image of himself). "That made me so sad to see you do a thing like that," (reflecting grief, not anger). The poor child's head was hanging lower and lower, as he felt guilt over giving his precious teacher pain. She then said, "I know that you aren't going to do anything like that again, are you?" turning up his little face to meet her eyes, "And we aren't going to talk about this any more," (smiling into his eyes and thus pledging that there would be no "gunny sacking" of this behavior to bring up as a constant reminder). The sadness on the child's face lifted, as he smiled back at her and went happily on his way to the center of his choice and to the rest of the day's activities.

We have said much about the important balance between **warmth** and **power**, because I feel it is one of the most important concepts one must master in order to shape children's behavior in a way that will be beneficial to them for life. Although this is not directly "spelled out" in the Bible, as we study God's Word it will be obvious that He has always shown great love and compassion (demonstrating warmth), but also has never been willing to leave us in our inappropriate behavior, for "whom the Lord loves, he also chastens," Pro. 3:12, Heb. 12:6 (demonstrating power).

"Yet indeed I count all things loss for the excellence of the knowledge of Christ Jesus my Lord, for whom I have suffered the loss of all things, and count them as rubbish, that I might gain Christ." Phil. 3:8

One approach to moral development that many consider to be totally secular is **Values Clarification.** In truth, the secularists consider everything to be relative, with no absolutes. For example, my valuing of being normal sexually as designed by God would be considered no better than the homosexual's valuing of homosexuality. In this sense, of course, values clarification is not useful for Christians. However, the seven questions that are asked in values clarification to determine whether something is a value to us, certainly will point out whether our Christian faith is truly valuable to us. If we were accused in a hostile environment of being Christians, would there be enough evidence to demand a verdict?

The questions, with appropriate verses from scripture, that we should ask ourselves to establish that our Christianity is important to us are as follows:

1. Is this something prized and cherished? A passionate love must be involved in order for something to be a true value to us.

   "I know your works, that you are neither cold nor hot. I could wish you were either cold or hot. So then, because you are lukewarm, and neither cold nor hot, I will vomit you out of My mouth." Rev. 3:15, 16.

2. Was this value chosen from alternatives?

   "I call heaven and earth as witnesses today against you, that I have set before you life and death, blessing and cursing; therefore choose life, that both you and your descendants may live." Deut. 30:19

3. Are you willing to publicly affirm this value?

   "Let the redeemed of the Lord say so," Psalm 107:2

4. Was this choice of value a free choice?

   "Behold, I stand at the door and knock. If anyone hears my voice and opens the door, I will come in to him and dine with him, and he with me." Rev. 3:20

   Are you aware of the consequences of this value in your life? Every value has its price.

   "Remember the word that I said to you. 'A servant is not greater than his master.' I f they persecuted Me, they will also persecute you. If they kept My word, they will keep yours also." John 19:20

5. Are you willing to do something about this value? It is not a true value unless you are willing to go beyond just talking about it.

   "Now by this we know that we know Him, if we keep His commandments."
   I John 2:3

6. Is this value consistent with other values held in your life?

   "Woe to those who call evil good, and good evil;" Isaiah 5:20

Although we may not want to take children through the values clarification questions, we as teachers should examine them closely to be sure that, indeed, we truly value our Christian faith above all other things. This is in order that we may be the role model for our children that flows from a heart totally dedicated to Christ. For children, more is "caught by example" when it comes to morality than is directly "taught."

An example of this is cited by William Preston from his memory as a child. His family was very poor when he was growing up, and William remembers that they were trying to sell a stove they had previously used in order to get needed money. The prospective buyers had agreed to the price, when William's father said, "I'm sure you noticed that the stove has a small hole in the back, near the bottom." The buyers had not noticed this, and they decided not to buy it. The father didn't make the sale, but he left a lifetime impression of the importance of honesty on his young son.

Sidney Simons, one of the major architects of values clarification has stated, "The values clarifier's function is to connect a person's creeds with his deeds." How much that is like our familiar statement that a Christian should "get his walk and his talk together!"

As Christians, the very fact that we value God's Word and Christianity means we could never agree with the values clarifier's stance that there are no absolutes. However, let us be sure that, with Paul, we can state that "all other things are rubbish" as compared with gaining Christ .

To summarize, Social Studies is all about helping the child to better understand his world, both the world close around him and eventually the far-flung lands around the globe, that he may learn to impact it for good. As the child learns about the world from God's perspective, it becomes clear that the environment should be protected because "The earth is the Lord's, and the fulness thereof..." and people should be cherished, "the world and those who dwell therein." Psalm 24:1 What a privilege we have as teachers to help children appreciate the beauty God has given to us in this world, and the opportunity to teach them to accept the responsibility of being stewards of this treasure for Him!

CHAPTER XI

Art and Music:
Appreciating the Beauty Around Us
While Soothing and Stimulating the Soul

"He restoreth my soul." Psalm 23:3

In an age that increasingly chases monetary gain, and runs faster and faster on the treadmill of life, secular schools are giving less and less time and space to the arts in their curriculum. Little do they realize their mistake, for God created us with a great appreciation of the beauty of His world and gave us organs of sight and hearing to nourish our souls, not just to earn a living. William Wordsworth summarized it well when he said:

"The world is too much with us; late and soon,
Getting and spending, we lay waste our powers:
Little we see in nature that is ours.
We have given our hearts away, a sordid boon!"

The youth of today is needing to "slow down and smell the flowers," as countless psychologists tell us. Perhaps the strange tendency toward depression in our country is partially because our children are not being taught to seek beauty in their surroundings, to create beauty for themselves and those around them, and to sing praises to God for His glorious creation. It is said that a child can begin to find beauty even in a slum if he/she learns to seek out the dandelion growing and blooming between the cracks in the sidewalk, rather than only concentrating on the gang graffiti that also surrounds him. On the other end of the economic spectrum, the rich children are "bored" to the extent of seeking out drugs for excitement, partially because they have not learned to creatively produce their own projects to express themselves for fun or artistic beauty.

Art and music are both part of the spectrum of appreciating and creating "to the glory of God." We will examine them separately, primarily to give specific academic uses for each, since that is sometimes what parents demand of the teacher. Nevertheless, they both feed into "restoring the soul" of each of us. The teacher also must allow time for personal creative pursuits in order to fully nourish the lives of children. We cannot give forth to others those characteristics which are not ours, particularly when it comes to values and serenity.

What is Art?

Beauty is, indeed, in the eye of the beholder. Therefore, we cannot hope to impose our tastes on children in art. What is needed is to open their eyes to the beauty around them, while also giving them an opportunity to see varying types of art that have been popular through the ages. If you are fortunate enough to be near a well-stocked art museum, this makes an excellent field trip. If not, fortunately there are numerous art posters, and even painting reproductions on the Internet. Gathering such a collection is considerably more trouble for the teacher, but once gathered these pictures will give a store of experiences for many years with only occasional updating. It is important to include various classic works, with a little information about the artist, as well as some of the more modern genre.

When I was in elementary school, I was part of an interesting school assignment one year. Since we lived in a city where the state fair was held, and the children received a day off for the fair along with free tickets to attend, the entire school was told to go to the art museum on the fairgrounds, look at all the pictures, then write down their favorite picture of them all. This required us to really look over the different productions and media, from watercolor to oils, etc., and think how they impacted us personally. I remember my choice, and can almost see the picture in my mind's eye today. Unfortunately, I do not remember the artist–I'm afraid he/she was not a famous one. I do remember it was a picture of children, an oil painting of unusual luminescence, so that it almost seemed to advance from the painting in a realistic manner. After we had all voted (and I'm sure some provision had to be made for those children who couldn't go to the fair, although I didn't realize it at the time), I was amazed to find that my picture was the most popular with the entire school! As I analyze it from an adult perspective, I believe it related to children because it was about children, and because it was vivid and realistic. They frequently respond most favorably to this type of art. Nevertheless, a show of hands (or, better still, secret ballots) indicating favorites in a classroom where you show a wide variety of art, will give children a chance to learn to appreciate some that were not their favorites. For third grade and above, the children could write a persuasive essay telling why their particular choice was best. At any age past kindergarten, the children could be challenged to make a persuasive speech to the class about their favorite painting before the ballot is taken, trying to convince others to vote for their choice. Who knows, we may be training a future salesman or a Christian politician (a practical defense to offer parents, as well). Our true goal, however, is to have children find beauty in many different art forms and in the world around them, so that their souls can be truly nourished.

Art is the Process, Not the Product

When working with young children in art, it is important to keep in mind that they should be encouraged to create what they want, not strive for some ideal as dictated by the teacher. Finger painting, collages, string painting, etc. are good examples of allowing children to experience colors and techniques without necessarily producing a recognizable product. In addition, it is important to include in the classroom those experiences which very few children will have in their own homes. Accordingly, a standing easel with newsprint paper and large paint brushes is an excellent investment. Young children may just want to practice broad strokes of color, or sometimes may paint over what to the teacher seemed like a lovely painting. When questioned, they may say, "It's dark now," as if they had been telling a time-related story with their picture.

Often if someone asks a young child about his painting, he will say, "I don't know. I'm not finished yet." As the child gets closer to being finished, a good thing to say, rather than, "What is that?" is "Tell me about your painting." It may then be desirable to print some of the words the child gives you at the bottom of the painting, as an important label for his work and a great pre-reading activity. When he takes his painting home, he will want to read his own words to his family about it.

Since art is the process, not the product, what about projects when the children all make an Easter basket to look exactly like the teacher's? Well, it means that these projects are not really art. They are not creative, but an exercise in following directions. This is not to say that such projects are without value, and frequently truly expected by both students and parents in preparation for such things as the Easter egg hunt. Following directions teaches listening skills, sequencing skills, and frequently goes along with a specific lesson in the curriculum. For these reasons, they are good activities. However, many teachers think that this takes care of art in the curriculum. It does not. The children must be allowed to create without a preconceived model for true art to be experienced. And that is the key–the creating process is the experience.

This doesn't mean the children have no parameters. Certainly, they should not be allowed to "be creative" by painting on the wall or their friend's paper. And, if their representations are inappropriate, it is best to discuss this with them privately, confiscating them quietly. Creativity must always be taught in the bounds of propriety, a rule that some of the current "artists" have ignored in situations like the case where a crucifix was displayed in a beaker of urine at a local art exhibit. This was thought by some to pass for "art" because art is "unbounded creativity." As Christians, we know that everything is about "freedom within limits." We can say with Paul, "All things are lawful for me, but not all things are helpful." 1 Cor.6:12

In Defense of Art

Parents who are eager for their children to be well prepared someday for the"best" of colleges and universities may oppose "wasting time" with the arts. Here are a few defenses that can validate academic outcomes from art.

Art can be a format for the teaching of academic information, from kindergarten, when children are learning about color names (reading and writing) and combining colors to make other colors (science) to upper grades when they make pottery as they study the life of the Native Americans. Art helps dry facts come alive and be vividly remembered by the children. How much do you remember that you learned by reading textbooks and answering the questions at the ends of the chapter? And, how much do you remember of those school projects which you put together creatively? The more children are involved, especially from a creative standpoint, the more vivid the learning, and therefore the more learning will be remembered. It is important, of course, that the teacher point out and emphasize the academic part of the art experience. It used to be thought that children should just be allowed to experience and discover their surroundings unaided. Naturally, researchers later found out that since the children did not have a name or explanation for what they had discovered, they soon forgot it, except to be somewhat curious. Teachers need to circulate during the art project for academic purposes and put labels on things by saying such things as, " Johnny is making a pitcher similar to the ones used by the Native Americans that we studied." "Mary has decorated her pottery with some of the hieroglyphics they used. Can someone remember what this sign means?"

An example of the need to label experiences comes from when I was a child in my bathtub. I loved to capture air in a plastic cup, force it down under the water, then tip the cup and allow it to come bubbling to the surface of the water. Nobody explained to me anything about air being lighter in weight than water, which caused it to come to the top. It was a wonderful experience, but I did not understand the meaning of it until much later. Even then, however, the vividness of the experience and curiosity about the process caused me to put it together with the scientific concept when I learned it much later.

Art can be a booster of feelings of self worth if handled appropriately, or a destroyer if used inappropriately. As long as all art work is displayed, without favoritism as to skill, children will delight in seeing their work spotlighted in the classroom. An easy way to make each painting seem special is to use slightly larger colored paper to put behind the children's drawing or painting to make it seem to be matted or even framed. Just be sure that all children's work is displayed at the same time or over a period of time. I still remember waiting and waiting for my picture to be put up where all could see it, then realizing that it wasn't going to be displayed because it wasn't good enough.

There is excellent research-based justification for encouraging creativity in children through art as well as in other ways. It has been found that children who learn to think "out of the box" in a creative manner, rather than only looking for the one correct answer or following the teacher's model perfectly, are far better problem solvers. A problem solver is the person who rises above all others in times of crisis, and this may be related to success in the business world for the parent who fails to see the value of creativity.

My husband is an excellent example of a man who refuses to be defeated when all practical means seem to have failed. He has always been creative in his thinking, and on one particular instance he helped me solve a not-too-serious, yet frustrating problem. We had traveled to another city to attend an educator's convention which was having a fancy evening banquet. I had purchased a new pantsuit that was very simple, but elegant. It was all black, and the main design feature was long, very full sleeves which had satin cuffs with rhinestone buttons. When I took it off the hanger, I popped the button off one sleeve. I was horrified! At that time, hotels did not supply sewing kits as so many do today, and I had not been wise enough to bring even a safety pin with me. I tried on the top without the cuff buttoned, and the super-full sleeve hung down past my hand when the cuff was not tight. It was hopeless. I prepared to just wear a suit I had worn to a business meeting, but my husband said, "Wait a minute. Let's see what we have here to work with." I had just purchased the pantsuit, and it still had the price on it. It was attached by one of those plastic tags with a "t" at one end which held the garment, while the other end was attached to the price.

The button had a shank on it, so my husband thought a while, then cut the plastic tag off the price, with a plan in mind. He next cut a short piece of this stiff plastic tag with his pocket knife, pushed it through the fabric of the cuff so that the "t" was holding it to the garment, ran the tag through the shank of the button, and I said, "But how are you going to hold it on the other side?" He smiled, pushed the tag through the fabric on the other side, then got the matches that were in the hotel ash tray (this was so long ago that hotels always still supplied ashtrays and matches). He lit one, and applied it to the end of the plastic tag, which melted into a ball. The button held securely, with the "t" on one side and the melted plastic ball on the other side holding it, and I got to wear my new pant suit!

I could tell you a lot to explain my husband's background in creativity, as compared to my own training in complete conformity. To keep it concise, I was always so afraid of failure in my parents' eyes that I only tried what I knew to be the safe and "right" method for doing everything. If I didn't know what that would be, I just was at a dead end. However, my husband was greatly left alone as a child to figure things out for himself, and he developed the technique of "playfully entertaining" all types of possible ways to solve problems instead of looking for only one right answer.

The point is, I could never have been the creative problem solver that he was and is. A great deal is in current teacher-research literature about the link between creativity and problem solving. If you have trouble convincing a parent, I feel sure you could find a current research-based article on the Internet to support this precept.

Music To Sing Praises to God

Music As a Mood-setter

Music both nourishes the soul and possesses practical implications. It can lead the children to associate pure joy with your classroom. Whether calmly soothing or vigorous for spontaneous dance, choose music that has joyful tones, not minor keys or "eerie" music (unless you have a specific lesson that calls for that). Perhaps you are aware how much "mood music" affects you in a film. The musical soundtrack of a film prepares you to be excited, calmed, romantic, sad, apprehensive, etc. If you haven't paid particular attention to the mood-setting effects of the soundtrack of a film, listen carefully and you'll see what I mean.

To begin with, music is a mood-setter that will set a cooperative tone for your classroom from the time the child arrives until the end of the day if it is used properly. Playing soft, quieting music as the children arrive will have a calming effect over any rowdiness that may have started in the halls or car pool. As you greet them warmly, it will help you to encourage each child to become involved in whatever arrival activity you have planned.

And it is very important to have plans for this "sponge time" between the arrival of the first child and the formal beginning of the day. For the kindergarten and perhaps first grade, you may want to set out wooden puzzles or other activities that don't take too long to put away, since this is for a brief period of time—usually about 15 minutes. As the children get older and are able to read, you may have an assignment written in a special place on the board where they know to look each morning as they arrive. This teaches the discipline of routine and getting down to work upon arrival. Children also derive security from routine, and they like to be able to predict what they are expected to do each day. In today's rushed and frequently insecure world, children need the calming effects of routine and soothing music to help them cope with other stresses they may be facing. And this classroom management technique will save you much stressing out yourself, as the children come in quietly instead of producing an ever-building level of noise.

If you do have a rest time in your classroom, either on rest mats or with the children simply putting their heads down on their desks to rest briefly after playground or other vigorous activity, playing quiet, soothing music also has a great settling influence. This is also helped by the teacher walking quietly around the room, smoothing hair and touching cheeks gently of those who are having a hard time settling down. It is important to walk slowly and quietly in order to add to the quieting influence.

Music can also set the tone for things that might otherwise be opposed by the children. Cleanup is one of those times. Of course, the first thing to do in order to prevent rebellion against stopping activities for cleanup is to train the children that you will always give them a five-minute warning before they will have to stop. This respects their need to "tie up loose ends" on whatever they are doing. It shows basic respect for the child and his work. Then, when I taught kindergarten, I taught them the little clean-up song that I made up, "Clean up, clean up, everybody everywhere. Clean up, Clean up, everybody does his share." You can set this to any familiar tune or make up a tune yourself. Then, after the five-minute warning had been given and the time arrived, I would just start walking around the room singing this, the children joining in and beginning to clean up. It really is amazing what a natural effect it has.

Years ago I was privileged to see the legendary Ella Jenkins (I think some of her records of music for children are still available) work in front of a huge audience with a group of kindergarten children she had never met before. She was a very large, loving black woman, and she had complete control over those children without ever moving from her chair. She did it through the enchantment of music. She introduced the children to rhythm instruments (which some of you may know can invite chaos if not handled carefully) in a beautiful, encouraging, but organized way. But what amazed me the most was how she, without having instructed the children in advance, managed to get the instruments returned to her and the children seated in a large circle. After they had marched around in a circle and enjoyed playing the instruments, she held out a large cardboard box and began to sing, "Put your instruments away, don't make a sound. Put your instruments away, don't make a sound." Then, "Put your instruments away and sit right down. Put your instruments away and sit right down." And, lo and behold, they did!

Academic Defense for Music

If you have a piano in your room, you may enjoy having the children respond to a certain chord you play on the piano to indicate time for specific routines. This is a good listening exercise, as the children come to differentiate between the chords and associate them with the correct activity. This, of course, will take time to teach. But it can be made into a fun game by playing a chord and saying, "Who can remember what this chord means?" etc. Listening activities are great pre-reading and early reading activities. This is just one of the many academic applications of music.

In addition to attentive listening, children can be taught the echoing of patterns of rhythm in music. If you have several soft-topped drums, these may be passed around and shared, or each child may bring an oatmeal box or plastic-lidded coffee can from home (or two if they have them) to make makeshift drums. The teacher will beat out a rhythm such as "long, long, short, short" and ask the children to repeat the same rhythm back to her. At first, teach them to do this as a class, then call on volunteers to repeat a rhythm individually until all are comfortable doing so. As they become comfortable with the simple rhythm, make up more challenging rhythms for them to repeat. This is good for math, and can even be used to teach fractions if you choose to introduce children to the quarter note, half note, and whole note on a musical staff. It also teaches auditory discrimination and auditory memory, which are so important for beginning readers.

Children also can learn to listen for analysis of pitch (Does it go up or down in the piece?) They can listen for dynamics: how the piece becomes louder or softer at certain times. A good recording to analyze is the orchestral "Peter and the Wolf," which helps the children to notice the sudden loudness when the wolf is introduced, and the gentle, gay tune that is played when Peter comes on the scene. Ask them to tell you how these different representations make them feel about what the wolf and Peter are really like. This work is a great one to study before an opportunity to take a field trip to visit an orchestral presentation for children if you are fortunate enough to live near such enrichment. If not, the sounds and names of various instruments can be taught by holding up the picture of each instrument as it is played on the recording.

Teaching concepts, such as colors, shapes, and safety to kindergartners and dates of historical events for older children, makes the learning much more vividly retained. Because music is not experienced on the same side of the brain as the side for learning words or reading, if we put them together it will cause both sides of the brain to be active at once. Much is currently being written about the integration of both hemispheres of the brain. This greatly facilitates retention of learning. Think about facts you learned by singing them at an early age. One date I have never forgotten is the result of a song I learned in grade school which said in part, "In fourteen-hundred ninety two, Columbus sailed the ocean blue."

Math instruction, as mentioned earlier, is enhanced by having fractions and musical notes for one eighth, one-fourth, one-half, and whole values. There are records and games set to music that teach mathematical concepts. This makes leaning fun, and, as previously said, much more indelibly retained. The children can learn the time signature, where the top number represents number of beats per measure and the bottom number represents the type of note that receives one beat. Have children clap out the rhythm of musical pieces you play for them, or march in time to the music. This can be pure joy, while also teaching them auditory discrimination, auditory memory, and reproducing responses.

Also, never forget to tell parents that too much stress leads to an inability to learn, therefore, the creative arts, by nourishing the soul, also sharpen the intellectual skills. Music and Art should never be made to serve only the academic part of the children. However, since some parents may insist that such subjects are only "wasting time," I have tried to explain some defenses to use with those parents.

If you are teaching in a Christian school, take every opportunity to mention to the children that we sing and make music to glorify God and to express our thanks to Him for all that He has given us. Similarly, as we create artistic beauty, it is a reflection of the beauty that He has given us inside our hearts, and our outward creations are a tribute to His goodness.

God is, indeed, the greatest of artists. His creation is marvelous indeed, and one of the primary artistic teachings that we have the responsibility to experience with children is to help them look for the beauty that surrounds them. Everyone can be taught to look for the colors of the sunset and enjoy them. A Ziggy cartoon shows Ziggy standing at an art easel looking at such a sunset and saying, "He does good work, doesn't He?"

Finally, as we use music to bring a thankful spirit of praise into our children's lives, and art to celebrate the beauty that surrounds us, we have made major strides in defeating the depression that psychologists tell us has become epidemic among even elementary school children. We often worry about teenagers, as we well should, but depression can occur much earlier than teenage. One of my college students told me that when she was five years old, she tried to hang herself. She got on a box to put her chin over the clothesline and hold on until she would be dead. What she didn't realize was that when she became unconscious her chin would be released, and she fell to the ground without accomplishing her awful mission. What a blessing that failure to kills herself was, as she was a wonderful student and has gone on to be a wonderful teacher! But few people realize that children that young can have suicidal thoughts.

Scientific studies have shown that a feeling of thanksgiving cannot coexist with feelings of depression, as previously mentioned, so we have a double reason for helping children to feel and express their thanksgiving for the beauty in their lives—God mandates it, and, as frequently is true with His mandates, there is a reward. In this case, the reward is to overcome a spirit of depression, which truly is used for great damage by the Prince of Darkness.

CHAPTER XII

Discipline and Classroom Management: Part A Planning To Prevent Problems

"For God is not the author of confusion but of peace," 1Corinthians:14:33a

No matter how sincere your motives in teaching, how accurate your goals, and how creative your teaching plans, the fact remains that if you cannot organize your classroom well enough to get the students to be quiet and pay attention, it all comes to nothing! Classroom organization and management, and especially student compliance with basic classroom rules, form the cornerstone on which classrooms stand or fall. I have seen many well-meaning teachers leave the classroom simply because they did not understand a few basic principles. Primary among these is a recognition that firmness is not only a kindness to the students in the long run, but also essential to a successful teaching environment. Scripture tells us that, "foolishness is bound up in the heart of a child;" Prov. 22:15a. As a result, children seem to have an innate desire to challenge and, to their own detriment, throw over rules if the authority figure will allow them to do so.

As an illustration from my own first year of teaching Kindergarten, let me tell you a little story. I had taught seventh and eighth grade previously before returning to the university to become certified in Early Childhood Education, and had learned there that discipline was of paramount concern at that grade level. Nevertheless, I thought that working with very young children would be different. Partly due to an extremely liberal bent in my university preparation, I had become temporarily "brainwashed" into thinking that all I had to do was encourage the young children, and they would be glad to obey me. I don't know why I forgot the basic nature of man that the Bible teaches, but I had temporarily set that aside. I knew I needed the children's attention during my direct teaching sessions, but I erroneously felt that they should be able to interact in centers with almost complete freedom (as long as they didn't hurt one another). The noise level was driving me crazy, but I made up my mind to tolerate it "in the best interests of the children." Then, one day, I saw one of my little children with her hands over her ears, and I realized that the noise level was too high for many of the children, as well as for me! As I gradually tried to institute needed rules (some four or five weeks into the semester), I discovered that, in the absence of my having established rules at the first of the semester, the children had established their own rules and looked upon me as "mean." when I tried to change them! Silence had given consent in a number of areas where I had failed to stop inappropriate behavior when it first occurred. I struggled with the children's behavior for most of the rest of that year! Nevertheless, I learned several valuable lessons from the experience. First, I learned that the primary thing a preschool teacher needs to teach for the first two or three weeks is what the rules are, why we have them, and what procedures (such as lining up to go to lunch, etc.) are necessary for the classroom to operate effectively. Secondly, I learned that rules, once carefully explained and established, need to be lovingly but firmly enforced. The teacher should demonstrate an attitude of sadness at having to enforce them (as opposed to the "I gotcha" technique of some uncaring teachers), but repeat why it would be impossible to have class if we didn't have necessary rules and procedures. Later in this chapter, I'll go into how to establish these. Thirdly, I learned that firmness is kindness. It is kinder to prevent inappropriate behavior from the first than to allow or even encourage bad habits to develop which will cause the children trouble, often for the rest of their lives.

Teaching in higher grades differs from the above only from the standpoint that these children have experienced classroom routines before. However, rules still must be established firmly with them for your classroom at the first of the year. It is a well-known fact that in schools where children travel to several different teachers in the course of a day, the same class will have perfect (or near perfect) classroom behavior for one teacher and appalling classroom behavior for another. That previously mentioned "foolishness in the heart of a child" causes them to "test the waters" to see what they can "get by with" doing in each class. Look upon that testing as part of the learning environment, and firmly but calmly remind them of the rule and the reason for the rule. Or, even better, ask the children, "Who remembers the rule that Johnny is forgetting? Why do we have this rule?" And, by the way, if you can't think of a reason that the children can understand why a rule is needed, get rid of it. Unfortunately, we should not have rules in the classroom that benefit only the teacher (like long periods of quiet and inactivity while she grades papers).

One teaching principle that is necessary for the teacher who would establish organization and discipline in her classroom is to model those virtues. The teacher who can never find anything on her desk when she is looking for it serves as a very poor role model for encouraging the children to be neat and orderly with their own work. Likewise, the teacher who becomes loud, angry, and somewhat out of control when children are out of control (sometimes with the notion that this anger will get their attention), is a poor role model for demonstrating self-discipline to the children. And that, after all, is our ultimate goal in discipline. We want to teach them how to have freedom through control. Nobody is truly free if he allows passions to be in control. Proverbs 16:32 reminds us, "He who is slow to anger is better than the mighty, and he who rules his spirit than he who takes a city." If we can help our children along the road to realizing this principle, it will be of greater value than any subject we might try to teach. As important as it is to teach a child to read (and I am a great proponent of this essential!), learning to control self will and diplomatically deal with opposition is truly of greater value.

Montessori, the famous early childhood educator previously mentioned, held up self discipline as an objective literally transcending any particular academic or social goal. She stated that the child who WILL NOT tie his shoes is just as handicapped as the child who CANNOT tie his shoes. Deeply religious herself, the Golden Rule was her foremost operational principle. She believed that this type of training for the child was the hope of a world based on self control, order, and the common good. Many current Montessori schools have emphasized her belief in the "liberty of spirit," while failing to notice that all of her writings indicate that freedom should be limited by the needs of other children or adults. She clearly subscribed to policies which discourage children from offending others. However, Montessori planned an active, child-involved program. She wisely stated that the child must come to know early the difference between good and evil, but good must not be seen as immobility and evil as activity. This tendency to equate any type of activity with evil unfortunately is still prevalent in many educators today.

An Ounce of Prevention: Indirect Discipline

Much has been written about how to control inappropriate behavior, and I will deal with that issue in Chapter XIII. However, I first feel the necessity of talking about what is called "indirect discipline." Basically, these are strategies that help to prevent trouble, or, in the popular vernacular, ways for the teacher to prevent "shooting herself in the foot." Discipline problems will occur in even the best-planned classrooms, but there is certainly no reason to do things (or fail to do things) that will naturally bring chaos into your classroom!

First of all, have a good plan for where you are going (your objective for the students to learn from the lesson) and several creative ways to arrive at this destination. Thus, if Plan A seems to be leaving the children restless and disinterested, you have Plan B ready for a quick switch. This doesn't mean that the children are in control, it means that you are always scanning your group to determine whether or not they are tending to become restless. This doesn't mean just the children who always have trouble paying attention; you can deal with them individually. But at the first sign of a generally attentive child losing eye contact with you, it's good to begin to evaluate whether the method is perhaps not an effective one, at least not for this class at this time.

Some teachers make the mistake of saying, "I will make them learn to pay attention, whether they are interested or not!" While this may prove your power and control over the group. It doesn't do much for instilling the love of learning in children. If they exit your class loving to learn, they are on their way to joy in the lifetime of learning that will be necessary for them to continue to be educated young people and adults. If they leave with the perception that learning is something to be endured until they can escape from it, the teacher has done them a great disservice.

In addition to having multiple plans of action, it is also important to plan more than you think you can accomplish in a daily session. Sometimes just "picking up the pace" can invigorate children and keep them interested and attentive. In this case, you may find that you will need more material than you had thought. Above all things, you don't want to "run out of soap," particularly if you are a beginning teacher. Veteran teachers have a better sense of how to pace a lesson, and also a better repertoire of "sponge" activities to insert if the lesson goes more quickly than they had anticipated. However, for a beginning teacher, it can strike a note of terror to realize that you've done everything you had planned and there is still ten minutes remaining! This is true for almost any new task. I once had a preacher who started his ministry straight from his life on the farm. He often preached to the cows he was milking in order to practice his sermons. On his first sermon in the church, he commented much later that he had preached to the cows about it for over thirty minutes, but somehow when he got into the pulpit it only lasted ten minutes and then he then realized he couldn't think of anything else to say! So, plan and have the materials to present much more than you think you will be able to accomplish each day.

One of the things you don't want to forget is to have needed materials lined up and ready in advance. I always liked to do this the afternoon before, rather than waiting until early the next morning. Perhaps you are one who prefers to arrive extra early to do this, but I have found that the time at the end of the day is yours to extend as long as needed, whereas the time at the beginning of the day may be interrupted by some need of the principal or another teacher, and it is, of course, limited by the time of the children's arrival. In either event, one thing to consider is materials shared by other teachers. If there is a filmstrip or book or any other materials that are shared among teachers, it is extremely disconcerting to find at the last minute that another teacher has it down the hall!

Time is Important: Schedule It Wisely!

Time should be scheduled carefully. This doesn't mean being inflexible with situations that arise, but "if you aim at nothing, you hit it every time." A great deal of time will be wasted if the day is not well planned. You should stick with a fairly consistent schedule, since children derive much security from routines and the ability to predict what is coming next. This is all an important part of their learning self-regulation, and therefore a key part of that "hidden curriculum" which may actually be more important than specific daily learning.

At the beginning of the day or class period, there is usually a time span of about ten minutes or more while the children gradually filter into the classroom. Trust me when I say that if you don't have scheduled and communicated plans for that interim time period, you will lose control of your class before it even begins! If you are teaching preschool, have planned materials such as easy puzzles or paper and crayon materials available so that you can direct the children to them quickly as they arrive. Just be careful not to allow such activities as getting out the larger blocks or other choices that will call for lengthy clean up. These short-term activities are known as "sponge activities," because they can be extended or shortened at will when you are ready to begin the scheduled goal plans for the day. You don't want to have to spend another ten minutes cleaning up after them.

It is well, especially with very young children, to alternate active and quiet learning in your plans. It has been proven that preschoolers' muscles are growing so rapidly that they actually may endure cramps in the muscles if kept sitting too long. As a matter of fact, haven't you even found as an adult that you become restless and achy when sitting still for an outstandingly long lecture? Therefore, also with older children, plan "stretch breaks." It is true that when they are totally involved in what they are doing (frequently from a self-chosen project), the attention span of even very young children is much longer than the old adage of approximately one minute per year of age. This is, again, a matter of reading your feedback. Your eyes should constantly be scanning the group for indications that it is time to change activities, take a stretch break, or perhaps switch to Plan B. As the year progresses, if you have done a good job of presenting interesting materials and not over-taxing their attention spans, you will indeed find that these attention spans have lengthened. At the beginning of the year with preschoolers, choose short books that call for interactive responses from the children. Gradually move to longer books, and if you find that you are losing them, don't be afraid to stop and say, "Boys and girls, I think that's enough of this book for today. Tomorrow I'm going to ask someone to tell us what we read today, and then we'll continue." And, you will nearly always have at least one child who is more mature and will be able, with help from you, to summarize the previous day's reading. This will instill a great sense of accomplishment in those children, and perhaps be an incentive to others to listen more carefully in the future.

Although you are the one to decide what activities are appropriate and effective for your group of children, it is wise to allow more than one method for the child to reach an educational goal. This way he will be more apt to claim "ownership" of the learning. For instance, after reading a book the child might choose between writing a traditional book report, making an oral presentation to the class entitled "Why I Think You Should Read This Book," or creating a diorama illustrating a major scene or scenes from the book. These dioramas might be placed in the classroom so that others may be attracted to reading the book. Actually, shoe boxes make great settings for dioramas, and things as simple as empty spools of thread can be creatively used to represent furniture or parts of characters. If you feel the children need practice in their writing skills, perhaps they could write a brief summary of the story, and then create an alternative ending for the book. They could then defend which ending they prefer and why. These alternatives may help alleviate the complaint of the child who says, "I'm not going to read another book because I don't want to write another book report!" The purpose of a book report SHOULD be to share with others the delight of having read the book. Too often, however, it turns into an attempt by the teacher to prove the child truly read the book. Let's be honest–it doesn't accomplish this goal. There are too many places, even on the cover of the book itself, to receive enough information to get by with writing a book report. Or, the book report may be an attempt to provide additional experience in writing. This is, indeed, a worthy goal. But a more creative writing assignment, such as planning an alternative ending, analyzing five types of people who would probably like this book and five types of people who might not and telling why, or writing a newspaper column advertising the book, would accomplish the same purpose using higher level thinking skills, and without the tedium of standard book reports.

We have previously talked about the calming effect of routines. For this reason, as well as for producing a more smoothly running classroom, there should be a general class schedule that is followed the majority of the time. During my first classroom at the preschool level, I erroneously believed that "variety is the spice of life," and I was excited about bringing change into the classroom. I was dismayed to hear children say, "Teacher, Teacher, we forgot _____ (the activity which usually came next)." They had security in being able to remember and predict what came next and were distressed when it was not so. This is less crucial with the upper grades, but at any level it is wise to stick to routine schedules except for special occasions, and then to tell the children about these changes well in advance. This will help to build excitement about the special days in advance, and can also lead to calendar activities for the younger grades to count the remaining number of days until the special day will arrive.

Transitions Can Make or Break Your Classroom!

An area that beginning teachers frequently find difficult concerns the necessary methods of transitioning from one activity to the next. If everyone is allowed to change at once, such as when it is time to pick up their work for the day and line up for dismissal, the effect is usually chaos. But how, you may ask, can we be fair to everyone without letting them all proceed at the same time? Early in the semester, it is wise to get the children used to a variety of techniques for sequencing this. When children are first starting to learn their colors, the teacher may say, "Everyone who has on green today may pick up their materials and line up for dismissal." Then, proceed with other colors until everyone has had an opportunity to be called. Or, when phonics are being learned, the teacher could say, "If your name rhymes with cat, you may get your materials and line up." (This would be in a class where there were such names as Pat and Matt.) Or, "If your name begins like 'star', you may..." (Usually there are several names that begin with "s".) You certainly could creatively work out ways to review whatever your teaching for the current period has been.

For older grades, you might even let it be somewhat of a contest related to remembering materials just taught. A good teaching and testing technique is the EPRT method, which stands for Every Pupil Response Technique. The easiest form of this is the "Thumbs Up" version. Giving the answer to a question about material studied, the teacher may say, "If this is correct, give me a 'thumbs up.' If it isn't correct, give me a 'thumbs down.' If you aren't sure, give me a 'thumbs to the side.' " The teacher can then easily read the feedback of whether the students have grasped the material or not. This is a good pre-test for whether to spend additional total class time on some materials, versus whether a small group should receive extra emphasis on this material instead. Additionally, a teacher might let those who choose the correct response be the first ones to get their materials (always in an orderly manner) and line up. A more advanced form of EPRT requires an investment in small slates for each student. A short-answer question is asked, and the students write their answers on their slates, then place their slates at chest level, facing the teacher. Again, those with the correct answer might line up first while the concept is being patiently re-taught to the other students.

In a standard classroom, there are always times which can easily be allowed to become "trouble spots," or at least wasted time. These are such times as lining up and waiting for the bell to ring, lining up while waiting for car-pool pickups, or lining up while waiting to get a drink of water, go to the restroom in small groups, etc. In any of these situations, pushing and shoving easily develops if not countered by some methodology. Of course, close supervision by the teacher is the clue, but it is much more advantageous to also use this time as instructional time. These periods should not be more than about five minutes, so they lend themselves perfectly to "skill-drill" type activities. Such activities are ideal for reviewing or reteaching memorized materials like addition and subtraction facts, multiplication tables, consonant beginnings and rhyming in words, the words on a spelling list, capitols of states, presidents of the United States, etc. When these are presented in a game-like format, they keep the children's attention from wandering to more disruptive things, while also using the time for effective review. Research has proven that such rote memory learning can be practiced with good effectiveness for short periods of time (like these periods of having to wait in line), while they become dull and boring if practiced for longer periods.

Transitioning to center activities must also be carefully planned. This can probably be best accomplished by the use of a planning board. For the non-readers, pictures of the centers can be used. For each center, plan in advance how many children can work effectively, then have that many places available for choice. Younger children could have name cards which they hang on a set number of hooks for the center. If the hooks are all filled, they know to choose another center. For older children, there might simply be numbered slots on a list after the name of each center, where the children could write their names. This would give the teacher an ongoing awareness of how long students were spending in each of their choices. And choice is a major decision with centers. It is important to allow students to have some choices in their academic learning as well as in other areas, otherwise we risk bringing up young adults who will always wait to be told what to do (and perhaps by ignorant or even wicked leaders). However, it is also important not to let the immature student be in charge of more of his learning than he is mature enough to handle. Accordingly, it is ideal to work out some type of balance between student choice and teacher direction, based on the maturity level of the students. Some teachers devise a system whereby they assign the students to centers of the teacher's choice perhaps three days each week, allowing the students to choose one day a week, and on Fridays allow free choice of the centers if the children have already completed the work assigned by the teacher for them in centers for the week.

Each center should have instructions, even the centers for non-

or beginning- readers. These younger children should have what is called "command cards," which briefly give instructions for each center through rebus reading (remember—a combination of easy sight words and pictures). With these younger children, a complete explanation of what is to be done at each center should be briefly given by the teacher on the first day of each week, and careful teacher monitoring and circulation to answer questions is required.

When and how to leave the centers is also a transitioning problem. For beginning students who have not experienced centers and have little control, each group of children may all move from center to center in a designated sequence at the time a bell or other signal is sounded. This is an example of maximum teacher control, best used in classes that are very young or who have demonstrated that they do not respond well to freedom of choice. The disadvantage of this method is the fact that all children do not truly need the same amount of time in each center. Some will grow bored and restless, while others will feel frustrated and rushed by such a schedule. Therefore, it is advantageous as soon as possible to carefully teach students how to finish their work in a center, where to put the work when finished, and how then to proceed (with their card) to another center where there is an opening. Also, when it is almost time for the centers to be closed, the teacher should give a five-minute warning that the children need to be finishing their work and preparing to clean up the centers. This can prevent many a "meltdown" that sometimes occurs when children who are totally involved in their work unexpectedly discover that they have to stop immediately. This is more common with younger children, but children who have learning difficulties, though difficult to get involved in their work at times, can also be extremely resistant to moving on, once they are totally involved. In short, it boils down to the fact of mutual respect that is so important in the classroom. The children must learn to always treat the teacher with respect; but you, the teacher, must also respect their needs. Giving a warning before a bell is about to ring or before they must clean up their centers is showing your respect for them.

Another transitioning problem comes when there is no longer time to begin another center, the children have completed their work in their chosen center and cleaned it up, but it is not quite cleanup time. Again, these short lengths of unassigned time can quickly wreak havoc on your classroom if you do not have a plan. So, take the time to teach the class what to do during this period of waiting. In kindergarten, I used to tell them to go to the library center, look at books, and sit on the carpet (waiting for the large group time which would be held in that area). It is important to have a "sponge activity" (as previously described) that will occupy them, yet be quickly terminated when the large group is ready to move ahead. When I taught eighth grade, I told them to always have a library book to read at their desks when they finished their work early. My eighth graders countered with the fact that the small school did not have a library, and that many of them lived in the country, rode the school bus, and could not get to the public library to check out a book. Not to be outdone, I brought a private collection of my own books from my childhood and teenage years, and formed a classroom library. Although I originally did this to prevent any from saying that they couldn't find anything to do (but bother their neighbors), it turned into a very important way of allowing the children to experience books that they would not have been able to access, since there was no available library. I also taught some of the children to function as library assistants in checking out my books to the students who wanted to take them home. I was warned by some of the more negative faculty members that I would gradually lose all my books, but I am proud to report that they were wrong, and I did not lose a single book. Students tend to live up (or down) to our expectations of them, and I had demonstrated respect for them by trusting them with my own books. They responded by demonstrating respect for me in taking special care of the books and returning them.

Organizing the Room for Efficiency and Order

The room itself says something to students (also parents and other guests) about what type of order is expected. Desks and work areas should be neat and carefully grouped. Trash and other clutter should be eliminated each day. Areas for relaxing reading should be warm and inviting, yet clearly visible to the teacher at all times. Strive to create a businesslike but inviting atmosphere. For example, young children frequently would rather lie on a carpet in the reading center to read their books than take them back to tables or desks. Some teachers provide antique bathtubs on legs with pillows inside to make reading seem more fun to the children. Reading nooks or lofts may also be used, but with the important provision that all parts of these should be clearly visible to the teacher at all times. True, every child likes to find a special "hiding place," and such arrangements can be very cozy. However, the possibility of undesirable behavior occurring in these cozy nooks outweighs the desirable variables. As the teacher, it is your responsibility to be monitoring everything that is going on in your classroom at all times.

Plan your classroom in such a way that there are clear areas for traffic to move without congestion. For instance, classroom student storage lockers or places for work to be picked up should not be too close to chairs or other classroom equipment. Keep frequently used materials easily available for both students and the teacher, while seldom used materials should be stored out of sight neatly in cabinets. Be sure that all students can see instructional presentations and displays. And, as previously stated, make certain that the teacher is able to see all students at all times.

Tips For Scheduling a Successful Day

Always plan to arrive well ahead of your students. The peaceful composure necessary to weather the ups and downs of teaching can only develop when you arrive in time to "settle" yourself well about the day's plan before the children begin to arrive. After that, you will be ready to meet their needs and direct your attention to them, rather than trying to organize your thoughts about what you are going to do next.

After the children have all arrived, it's time to announce your plans to them for the day. Your goals should never be unknown, as if you expect them to find out on their own what you want them to accomplish (some teachers almost seem to make a guessing game out of this!). Early in the day or period, let the children know what you have planned for them to accomplish for that day. Then at the end of the time period, remind them of what they have accomplished (so, when Mom says, "What did you do today in school?" They won't say, "Nothing.") Also, repetition helps to make learning more permanent. There is an old saying that says you should, "Tell 'em what you're goin' to tell 'em; then tell 'em; then tell 'em what you told 'em."

In upper elementary school, you may choose to write these goals or assignments on the chalkboard in advance, but it is well to go over them with the children, since some may be non-readers or some may simply choose not to read them. Also, you will need to expand and explain the assignments, making sure the children understand them. In the upper grades it is especially good to have the condensed assignments on the board, as they may become somewhat complex, and the children may have difficulty in remembering them. For younger children, however, it is best to announce only one objective at a time in order to avoid confusion. It's simply a matter of expanding their ability to be self-regulating as they demonstrate the growing maturity that shows they are ready for it. Just as you wouldn't expect a baby to feed himself without help when he is a week old, you would also not be helping him to grow if you continued to feed him that way when he became a four-year-old. The amount of help provided for children to do their classroom assignments also changes as they grow in maturity. If you expect too much of them, they'll be confused and frustrated (and, by the way, if you see these signs developing, be aware that it is time to back up and proceed more gradually). If you continue to "spoon feed" them, they'll keep with the old routine, but they won't grow in their ability to be in control of themselves. Our goal in all teaching is to help children eventually come to the place where they will be self-regulated lifetime learners, motivated by learning rather than by the teacher, and able to proceed to learn in the areas of their own interest with little or no guidance. You may say that is a far distant goal, but it is good to keep it in mind as we encourage children to progress toward it. The good teacher is always trying to work herself out of being needed by the current set of children, knowing that new needy ones will be arriving by the next semester!

The demeanor of the teacher is extremely important in establishing respect and obtaining obedience in the classroom. Frequently, teachers who are unaware of this fact will accidentally, through their behavior, undermine all the good planning they have invested into organizing their classroom for success. Body language must be consciously controlled. Studies show that when a person exhibits one type of verbal language and an opposite type of body language, other people (and especially children) will tend to believe the body language. The image you want to project is one of in-control, business-like, confidence. The children will be more likely to follow your lead if they are sure you know what is the best thing for them and the classroom. An image of hesitancy dispels this confidence. Therefore, consciously plan to walk tall, calmly, and decisively when you move about the classroom. Look directly at the children, pausing to have them make eye contact with you. I used to say to my kindergartners, "Let me see your eyes." It's amazing how well this little saying works with preschoolers. Then, scanning to look each one in the eye consecutively, give the important announcement you need to make. Never ask for complete attention like this unless it is for something important you need to say. Then, looking at them seriously, use a carefully regulated voice for your announcement.

In all dealings with children, strive to make your voice animated and enthusiastic, with a firm, business-like manner which communicates that you expect obedience. In all transactions, keep the volume down. The children should get quiet in order to hear you, not expect you to speak louder over their chatter. Accordingly, you will need some type of signal to tell them to get quiet and listen to you. This is one of the procedures you will need to teach from the very first day. Some teachers flick the lights on and off. Others have a bell that they ring. In classrooms where there is a piano, a certain chord may indicate, "Be quiet and turn to hear what the teacher has to say." Some teachers, in an effort to get group cooperation and constant awareness of the children's need to check their surroundings, will have a hand signal (such as a raised hand with the palm toward the children) that they use. The first children to see the hand signal will turn to face the teacher, also displaying the hand signal, and gradually the other children will join until all are aware of what is going on. In the lower grades, this can be a real contest for who will see and pass the hand signal early and which children are caught at the very last. This gives the teacher the opportunity to praise those children who were paying close attention, and remind the stragglers (kindly) that although they were forgetting to watch this time, you're sure next time they'll remember and be among the first to respond!

Although I'll say more about this in the next chapter about responding to disciplinary infractions, it is important to mention here that the natural tendency of a person is to speak more quickly and with higher pitch when becoming the least bit agitated. That is a perfectly natural tendency, and may be helpful when it is necessary or desirable to indicate to someone that he is causing you to be distressed. However, as the leader of a classroom, it is important to demonstrate to the children that although their behavior may make you sad, it never causes you to lose control. A calm, low-pitched voice while speaking slowly and deliberately will have a calming effect on the situation. In contrast, speaking more quickly and at a higher pitch will escalate any agitation in the children themselves. I once had a student teacher who didn't really believe this would happen. She was a naturally rather excitable person. One day when I was supervising her and a problem arose between the children, I suggested that she go to the area and speak, quietly, slowly, and calmly, in a low pitch about what was happening and what should be happening. It was definitely a "staged" situation, since that would not be her usual way of responding, and she had been having a great deal of difficulty in calming her classroom down. She came back absolutely amazed at what she had considered to be an almost magical effect on the children!

Plan to stay on your feet most of the time. A comfortable pair of shoes makes a good investment for a teacher, because good teachers do not spend a lot of time sitting down behind their desks. A good teacher constantly monitors and circulates when she is not doing direct instructional teaching. During centers work or independent seat work, tend to walk to the areas where trouble has had a tendency to develop in the past. This is a technique known as "proximity control." If you need an excuse to not be obvious, retrieve something from that area, adjust the blinds, or something of this nature. You don't want the children to feel you are "out to get them." Just the fact of the teacher being near frequently encourages restless children to settle down and do what they already knew they should be doing! If this isn't enough, a quiet hand on the shoulder, with a whispered reminder of what to do will frequently keep the rest of the class from being bothered.

When presenting any type of instruction at any level, remember to constantly be scanning the group to assess whether or not they are really "with you." I have learned that this is also important at the university level, where I have taught for over twenty-eight years. Even adults begin to have their eyes glaze over or show signs of restlessness when they have been kept sitting too long. When I see this, I provide time for a break. Also, scanning the group will help you discern when they do not really understand what you have said. Particularly with new learning or with complicated material, it is frequently important to stop and say, "OK, somebody please summarize for me what we have been talking about." If there are mainly blank stares, say, "Well. I obviously have you all confused. Let me back up and re-explain, and then I want you to ask questions so that I can make the meaning clear." I can't emphasize enough how important it is to take the blame upon yourself for having not made it clear, rather than saying, as some teachers do, "Well, if you would just listen, you would be able to answer the question." That is not following the rule of mutual respect that is so important in every classroom. If you want them to respect you, and you have every reason to insist that they do, you must also be willing to go more than half way to show respect for them. Show the position of willingness to accept the blame by saying something like this to older students. For kindergartners, when you discover that no amount of making your voice animated, etc. is going to get them interested in a book you are reading (which may be too advanced for their interest), simply close the book and say, "I believe that's enough of that book for now. Let's proceed to (whatever is next on the schedule)." The attitude that, "I will MAKE them pay attention" never leads to real learning at any level, and often results in a breach of that important bond between teacher and student that helps students want to listen to what you have to say.

When students respond to you or voluntarily share with the class, it is important for the teacher to give them constant eye contact, nodding, smiling, and showing encouragement for their comments as being important to both the teacher and the class. Intermittent, encouraging comments may also be made when it is appropriate, in order to enlarge upon what they have said. As students feel encouraged to share or ask questions, you will develop a wonderful window into the minds of your learners, as well as finding that your lesson has been enriched by what each learner brings to share. On the other hand, it is true that in the very early years children may share something that is totally off the topic of instruction. In such a case, a comment is needed, like, "Johnny, it's really very interesting that your cat had kittens, and I want to hear all about it later. But right now, we're talking about the Pilgrims." At the upper grade levels, sometimes you will encounter a student who wants to monopolize the class. You may even see the other students rolling their eyes because "Mary is talking again." In this case, a diplomatic way to handle it is to say, "Mary, I'm proud that you really do know so much about this topic, but I think it's time to hear from someone else."

Working with Large and Small Groups

Before calling a small group to work, such as a reading group or special instructional needs group, the teacher must first be sure that seat work is well understood by the rest of the group. Circulate until all the children have settled into the seat work before calling out a group for special instruction. Those few minutes invested in getting the large group working independently will be well worth it, because otherwise your small group instruction will be constantly interrupted.

Before calling the next group, ask the children to raise their hands if they need help with their work. Circulate to those with raised hands. If you find a child who needs a great deal of help, tell him the first one or two things to do, and promise him you will be back with him in a few minutes. Then circulate to other students who have only a quick question. Many teachers make the mistake of spending ten minutes with the first child, while the rest of the class gets restless and into discipline problems because they can't go on with their work without a simple question being answered. Do, however, be sure to go back to help the original child more fully after the simple questions have been handled. And don't call the next small group until questions have been answered. It's a good idea to at least quickly scan the classroom to see what needs to be settled down before calling each subsequent group. The children will soon learn that you will answer their questions before and between small groups and therefore will feel less compulsion to interrupt your instruction. This won't be 100% true, but will greatly cut down on the interruptions. If a child does come up to you with a question, courteously ask him to try to do the parts of the assignment that he does understand, and you will be with him as soon as the small group session has ended.

If your school operates on a bell schedule, be well aware of the time so that you can warn the children about finishing their work and getting ready to proceed to the next class, lunch, the car pool etc. NEVER let the bell catch you in mid-sentence of a story you are reading (plan for appropriate stopping places and chances to recap with the children), instruction you are giving, or a lesson. If you keep your eye on the clock, you can do a quick recap of the learning and reminder of assignments, along with instructions for the children to ready themselves for the bell. This all goes along with having a well organized classroom, which demonstrates an appropriate role model for the children. The teacher should demonstrate a proper organization of classroom space, goals, and time. Much "incidental learning", such as how to be well organized, is more "caught" than "taught." And such "incidental learning" is often among the most important things we pass along to our children.

Setting the Stage for Behavioral Expectations

Probably the most important learning to establish during the first week of school is the identifying of rules and procedures. It isn't fair to be upset with a child who has broken a rule he didn't know existed. How would you like a policeman who pulled you over for driving forty miles an hour and told you that the speed limit was twenty-five, even though there were no signs to tell you this? He might say that anyone should be able to tell that in this area forty miles an hour was excessive, but you would probably still resent the whole issue. Similarly, you as the teacher may feel that Johnny should know better, but in truth he may not. In any event, don't take a chance that he may give this excuse. Establish and teach rules and procedures at the first of the semester, then pause to review them frequently with the children during the first few weeks.

Rules, by definition for this section, shall be considered to be guidelines for regulating conduct. What is appropriate conduct on the playground frequently is not appropriate behavior in the classroom. However, there are some rules, such as not intentionally harming other children verbally or physically, that are appropriate in every setting. Procedures, on the other hand, shall be used to refer to a particular mode of operation to be followed for completing assignments, etc. In an upper grade classroom, having a specific place to turn in classwork and homework, along with instructions for how to handle work turned in late, will be a procedure that will save the teacher much sorting and searching after class. Both rules and procedures are extremely important to the efficient operation of the classroom.

The first rules and procedures that the teacher must learn are the rules and procedures of the school. These must, in turn, be conveyed to the children. Surprisingly, some teachers are unaware of basic rules and procedures of the school shortly after they have been hired, and may get themselves and their students into considerable difficulty because of this. Make this your first order of business after being hired to teach in a particular school, because particularly in the case of the procedures, schools vary widely. What should a child do if he comes to school late? What is the procedure for having an excused absence, etc. There is usually a book somewhere that explains these procedures for the school, but it is wise to ask for it, since otherwise it may be overlooked to mention in your training. For professionals like teachers, ignorance is no excuse. You are expected to know the rules and procedures of the school where you have been hired to teach.

Be sure the children in your classroom know these school regulations along with what is forbidden, what the consequences are, and any administrative procedures. For younger children, teach them first the most important things that relate to them. Many of the regulations will either not relate to them or will be rare enough that you can talk of them later in the year. But help them to feel secure by knowing how to proceed when outside your classroom as well as when they are with you. For older children, they may already be acquainted with most of the rules and procedures of the building. However, there are always those who either are new to the school this year or who have never truly internalized rules and procedures in the past. For the sake of these, plan to go over the school regulations early in semester, perhaps asking the children to do most of the teaching for you, to keep the more knowledgeable children from being bored. "Who can remember one very important regulation in our school? (Pause for answer) Good for you! Susie, will you write that on the board for us, please, using your best penmanship?" Then continue in this vein until they have failed to come up with certain things, which you then need to add. Here, a few hints to help them remember will make it like "Riddle-a-Diddle" in the younger grades—a game, rather than just a dull rehashing of rules and regulations.

Rules for the individual classroom should be established as soon as possible. That means certainly before the end of the first week, and preferably on the first day. Sometimes school requirements for the first few days may preclude doing this at this time, but the emphasis should be on doing these as soon as possible before bad habits begin to develop and have to be "unlearned." If the children are old enough to help in establishing the rules, they may be asked, "What kind of rules do you think we need in order to have an orderly and pleasant learning environment for everyone?" This does not mean that you have to accept every rule they suggest, but take the time to lead them through why this might not be a good rule. Also, some of the rules they suggest may be too specific or too general, so they do not need to be adopted exactly as the children suggest. On the other hand, help the children to agree with the proposed changes, because if they feel they have had a part in selecting the rules, they will have a tendency to have "ownership" in them, and thus will be more ready to abide by them.

All rules should meet the "Three R's of Rule-Making: Reason, Respect, and Relevance." In addition, they need to be appropriate for the age group of the class. For instance, there probably is less reason for a rule about "keeping hands, feet, and possessions to yourself" in a sixth-grade classroom than there would be in a kindergarten classroom. However, if sixth-graders need such a rule, this would probably be an example of a rule that the teacher might call students together later in the semester and say, "After what happened today in the lunchroom, do you think we need to make a new rule?" Concerning "Reason," this means don't make unnecessary rules. Unnecessary rules will not have validity with the children, and will probably result in too many rules being made. It is important to keep the number of rules few, so that they will be readily remembered. The classic suggestion is not fewer than five, not more than eight. "Respect" should be the keynote of every rule: respect for other children, the teacher, and the classroom as a place for learning. "Relevance" indicates that the rules must be stated in a manner that the children can understand and agree to be important for their daily experiences.

After the rules have been made clear, it is important to teach them as thoroughly as one would teach the multiplication table. This means they should be automatic in memory, not something the children need to stop and ask themselves. At first, however, children will forget them, and it is important to take the time to stop and say, "Boys and girls, what rule is being broken here?" That's all part of the procedure of making rule learning permanent. Some of the rules may not be new to the children, but probably at least some of them will be. Remember, the rule of thumb for new learning is that it takes an average of twenty repetitions for the learning to be presented before it becomes permanent. That is important for teachers to realize so that we will "not grow weary in well doing, knowing that in due time we shall reap if we do not give up hope." (Gal. 6:9)

In addition to many repetitions of the rules, it is desirable to post them somewhere in the classroom. Later in the semester, it can be quite effective to have an offending student go to the list and point to the rule he is infringing. This is particularly true in classes who are able to read, but posting the rules and going over the printed form with non-reading children serves a good purpose, as well. As previously stated, people begin talking to babies at birth, long before the babies can understand the language, and the ones who are addressed the most usually develop their language skills earlier. Surrounding the infant with language before he can understand prepares him to gradually sort out the meanings of various words as he is ready to do so. Similarly, surrounding a non-reading child with print and talking with him about it, prepares those who are able to begin to notice helpful cues about print.

This chapter has been designed to give ideas about how to keep from causing discipline problems in your own classroom. Poorly planned or poorly handled class sessions can cause discipline problems. The last thing you want to do is cause problems, thus becoming your own worst enemy. Yet, it is absolutely true that in spite of your best plans and procedures, a child sometimes comes into the classroom as a "bomb waiting to explode." It may be something that happened in the car pool or at the breakfast table at home. Or, it may be situations you would be shocked to know about that are occurring in the home, such as all types of child abuse that are far too common. Those situations you couldn't prevent (although, in the case of child abuse you may need to report), but you will certainly have to deal with them. You'll also have to deal with the hyperactive child, the disrespectful child, and a host of other problems that children will bring into your well-organized, well-conducted classroom. The next chapter will suggest methods of dealing with these.

CHAPTER XIII

Discipline and Classroom Management: Part B Dealing with Misbehavior

"I will instruct you and teach you in the way you should go; I will guide you with My eye."Psalm 32:8

When a child is overtly misbehaving in your classroom, disturbing the other children and destroying the leaning environment, the teacher cannot afford to ignore it and just "hope things will work out." No, "silence gives consent," as researchers found who had advised teachers to ignore bad behavior and reward good behavior. The theory was that ignored behavior, because it was not reinforced, would disappear and be replaced by the good behavior that was rewarded. Well, maybe that works with rats (where most of the first discipline research began), but it doesn't work with children. In one preschool class, little children who were disadvantaged and uneducated, but definitely far above the level of laboratory rats, were observed saying to each other, "She don't say nothin'. It must be all right."

However, just what to do is not agreed upon between major theorists, or even among very effective teachers. I am going to give you a brief description of a spectrum of discipline techniques from which you can choose both the theory and the methods that best suit your personality, the age of the children, and the particular child and situation. It is important to keep in mind that your goal is not only to make misbehavior stop so that class can proceed, but also to help the child learn that such behavior is not in his own best interest. Therefore, think carefully about which types of discipline techniques are most effective. Perhaps you will feel that in some instances you will want to use one approach, while in others your approach will be from an entirely different part of the discipline spectrum.

Whole books have been written about the spectrum of discipline principles, along with an analysis of various discipline techniques and where they fit along the spectrum. Therefore, I will only be able to give you a rough outline of the framework. However, it should be enough to get you started toward forming your own special philosophy of discipline. The spectrum varies primarily in the amount of power that is given to the student to deal with his own behavior and the amount of power given to the teacher to control the behavior. Perhaps you are saying, "Why should I give the student power? He'll just run the classroom to suit himself, and then nothing will improve." No, there are not any effective discipline programs that would advocate that. Teachers, by their very job description, must set up the rules for the classroom, with varying amounts of input from students as indicated in the previous chapter. Those rules, then, must be enforced. However, they are enforced in varying ways, depending on the age levels of the children and the comfort level of the teacher with specific methods.

The discipline spectrum ranges from the "Counseling: Relationship-Listening" end to the "Teacher Control: Rewards and Punishments" end. As would be expected, the counseling end of the spectrum involves much more time with the student, sitting down with him and trying to get him to see why his behavior is going to cause him problems not only in the classroom, but in later life also. The rewards and punishment end of the spectrum utilizes what has been learned through research about positive and negative reinforcement of behavior. It is a more mechanical approach, but highly effective in proper habit forming, and certainly a speedier method of controlling behavior. There is a middle position of "Blended Control," where counseling is involved, but with a firmer hand directing the student toward the desired behavior. James Hymes, in his classic book on discipline entitled *Behavior and Misbehavior*, likens the teaching of proper control in the student to learning to fly an airplane. He contends that those teachers who use only teacher control techniques are saying to the student, "Now you sit there and watch me fly this plane, and later I'll turn it over to you." He thinks the extreme counseling approach is even more dangerous, saying those teachers are basically saying, "There's the airplane; now, go fly it!" The way that students actually learn to fly an airplane, of course, is with dual controls. The teacher is in control at first, but gradually releases more and more of the control to the learner, always standing ready to resume control if danger results from a learner mistake. That, says Hymes, is what teaching the child to control his behavior should be all about.

Now I have mentioned previously that the basic nature of the teacher will dictate to a large extent which type of discipline method she finds most acceptable. A teacher who has little tolerance for any type of classroom noise or disruption is going to prefer the structure of a teacher-controlled method. And if you truly need complete quiet and order, it is probably for the children's best interest that you set out to achieve them. There is an old saying that says, "When Mama ain't happy, ain't nobody happy." I think this follows in the classroom also, with the teacher. If you try to form yourself into the image of some other teacher you greatly admire who is very different from yourself, it frequently leads to disaster. God has made us as different as snowflakes, and He wants us to operate the way He created us, just seeking to be the best we were meant to be. I have seen very happy classrooms with high teacher control, and I have seen smoothly functioning, happy classrooms where there is much less teacher control.

Those teachers who are deeply into feeling the hurts and needs of the students, along with being willing to wait longer for results and put up with a certain amount of classroom disruption, may primarily prefer the counseling approach. Then, there are all types of positions in between the two approaches at the extreme ends of the spectrum. Your preference for blended control may lean toward more teacher control than counseling, or it may conversely emphasize more counseling with some teacher control. All positions have their strengths and weaknesses, and it is difficult to give you a cookbook solution to the problems arising in your classroom. Many discipline approaches try to do this, but it is better for you to understand the underlying beliefs behind each philosophy of discipline and decide what you truly want to do, rather than relying on an undifferentiated "bag of tricks" approach without knowing why these "tricks" may or may not work. It is not an easy task to determine which method to use in each incident and with each child. We may well join with the spirit of The Serenity Prayer and ask God to give us "the wisdom to know the difference."

The Counseling: Relationship-Listening Model

The Counseling: Relationship-Listening model is built on the foundation of student trust and respect for the teacher. If the students feel that you are their enemy rather than their friend, it will never work. First of all, they will not open up to you and tell you what is bothering them and could have been behind the misbehavior. In many instances they may not know what is the cause of their behavior, but if they trust you and understand that you truly want to help them, they may be willing to share with you what is happening in their lives. Then, it will be up to you to decide whether or not you can help them solve their problem. If it is a problem at home, unless it is true child abuse, about the best you can do is give them advice on how to cope with difficult situations and difficult people. Perhaps you can also help them to see the problem from the standpoint of their parents, who may be exhausted from working several jobs in an effort to give the child a better way of life. Perhaps it will just help the student be able to cope if you are available to listen to him on a regular basis.

This model is built upon the premise that nobody can truly "fix" a problem except the person who is experiencing it. The teacher will primarily act as a sounding-board and a buffer against further frustration while the child works out his own problem or problems. You may be able to understand this approach and relate to it if you have ever had a friend who sympathetically listened, encouraged, and advised you about a problem in your own life. You still had to solve that problem yourself, but it gave you confidence to know that someone you respected and admired believed in you and wanted to help.

Some of the commercial models that embrace this philosophy are the Supportive Model of Thomas Gordon, the Communication Model of Berne and Harris, and the Valuing Model of Raths and Simon. If you feel drawn to this type of discipline control, it would be a good idea to get some of the books which explain these models in order to glean some techniques from them. However, just taking the time to listen supportively and analytically to a troubled child will put you on the way to working out your own techniques for change.

Like all of the points on the spectrum of discipline and classroom management, Counseling:Relationship-Listening has its strengths and weaknesses. The major strength is the fact that only the person with the problem can truly come to the best solution of how to handle it (because only he knows all the details, as well as having the power to change himself). Also, it encourages the child to think more deeply and assume more responsibility for analyzing and changing his behavior because of realizing it is beneficial to himself to do so. When success is achieved by this route, the child becomes more self-confident of being able to tackle and solve subsequent problems in life. And finally, this approach is the best one for improving student attitudes, particularly for the child who thinks the whole world is against him.

The weaknesses of this model include the fact that it presupposes a certain amount of rational ability which may not be present in the very young (although it is in some) or in children who have never been helped to reason through situations in the past. It also presupposes enough verbal ability to share and understand. This, too, is limited by age and IQ. Additionally, as the critics of this approach are quick to point out, might not all the extra attention of counseling serve as a reward for unacceptable behavior? And, in a truly practical sense, does the teacher have this much time to spend on one student? My advice to you would be to pick and choose which students might be most likely to respond to this long-range approach, and use this technique selectively, rather than as your total classroom control program. Finally, the major weakness of these programs is that none of them give any instruction for how to deal with and put a stop to violent behavior.

The Blended Power Model

The Blended Power model is built around the concept of the dual-control airplane discussed earlier. Although the teacher starts off with rules and reminders to the student, she gradually expects the student to remember these things without prompting. It is also dependent upon the view that students best learn control by coming into contact with the needs of others and becoming more aware of how they would feel if someone did to them what they had just done to another person. It is a step away from the basic self-centeredness that we all possess at birth, moving toward an awareness of the needs of the world around us. The student is often requested to come up with a plan or "contract" for better behavior. He may even be asked what punishment should be enacted in the event that the contract is not fulfilled. All of this is putting responsibility upon the student, requiring him to come up with a plan for change and stick to it. The plan or contract must be acceptable, not only to the child, but also to the teacher and the other students. Sometimes the other children are even called upon to help remind the child (in a friendly and encouraging manner) about fulfilling his contract.

This method, along with the Counseling model, requires the foundation of respect and warm feelings between teacher and student. In any model for working out an agreement that is acceptable to both parties, if this element is missing there will be deception and mistrust. Many studies have concluded that a student's attitude toward the teacher is the greatest determinant of whether or not he will tend to modify his behavior according to the teacher's instructions, or even be willing to learn from the teacher. Also, it has been found that students who do not feel that the teacher values them personally will rarely interpret her suggestions as being in their best interests.

Those who are intrigued by this model might be interested in reading about the Social Model of Rudolf Dreikurs (who promotes the idea of "logical consequences"), or the Reality Model of William Glasser (where the student draws up a complete contract for future behavior). Even if you do not totally subscribe to one of these models, you should be able to glean some helpful techniques from their methods of classroom control.

Among the strengths of the Blended Control model is the fact that it avoids extremism from either end of the control spectrum. Children are not given more control than they can effectively handle, yet teachers don't make all the decisions about rules and consequences if these rules are broken. A major strength is that responsibility for appropriate behavior is placed upon the learner. He learns that it is not acceptable to have a "you (or my parents, or the other children) made me act irresponsibly," attitude. The responsibility for his behavior rests fully on his own shoulders. He can make good or bad choices when confronted with a situation, and he is led to understand how to make better choices in the future if he has behaved unacceptably.

The weaknesses of this model cited by critics include the fact that perhaps these "mutual plans" may actually be teacher plans to which the student feels required to agree. Also, since everything depends upon communication, what happens to the non-verbal student? Finally, could the use of the peer group to help with enforcement put too much pressure on the offender? Consider these possible weaknesses if you determine to use this type of program. A beginning mind set to avoid making the plans teacher-dictated, as well as avoiding the use of too much peer pressure, should prevent many problems.

The Teacher Control Model: Rewards and Punishments

This model is based on scientifically proven results of positive and negative reinforcement. It strongly subscribes to the belief that people are shaped by external stimuli more than by internal reasoning. Rules are made extremely clear at the beginning, along with the punishments that will occur when rules are broken. It is based on the scientifically proven fact that positive reinforcement (anything that the student finds desirable--which varies greatly from student to student), when offered after behavior occurs, will make that behavior more likely to be repeated. Also, anything that the student would like to avoid is known as negative reinforcement, and if these things occur after a student behavior, he will be less likely to repeat the behavior. This is a great oversimplification, since rarely is there only one set of circumstances present with the student for reinforcement. The class may give him much positive reinforcement when he is the class clown, even though the teacher may administer a negative reinforcement. Then, if he greatly desires peer approval, the teacher will need to help him find some other way to legitimately get this approval in class before he will stop being the class clown. Many specific programs from this model have carefully scripted ways of introducing the program (often by a letter to parents in addition to informing the children) and for handling situations that arise. This can be especially helpful to a beginning teacher who does not trust herself to "think on her feet."

Primary among these models is the Dare to Discipline Model of James Dobson. His model is more designed for parenting, so it has fewer specific suggestions for the teacher than the other models I will list, but it is an excellent example from many standpoints, primarily because of the Christian emphasis and the overriding principle that true love and discipline go hand in hand. Other major programs include the Behavior Modification Model, which is totally based on the use of positive reinforcement, and Lee Canter's Assertiveness Model, with its carefully scripted instructions for almost all situations needing control from the teacher before, after, and during transgressions.

The major strength of these programs is the fact that research has observably demonstrated that they do work in reducing the incidences of misbehavior. The programs therefore release more of the teacher's time for actually teaching curriculum. And they do not require a minimum level of cognitive or language ability in order for the child to understand. Also, it is important to remember that strong discipline, properly administered, is an indication of true love and respect, not the opposite of them. As teachers, we form a boundary of strong rules to protect the child's development because we do love and respect him.

The major weakness of the Teacher Control Model involves the question of whether this method only changes symptoms (overt behavior), but does not change root causes of behavior, which may come out in other ways. Relationships (as between teacher and child—which are so important in the classroom) are not established by rewards. Rewards are better used to reinforce training or habits. Also, are these methods actually in the best interest of children, since they are not working to teach the child to think through and control his own behavior rationally. And finally, many, such as the Canter Assertiveness Model, have only one carefully scripted method for all age levels, which may not be effective for all ages of children.

If rewards are to be used, research has shown us that the use of intermittent rewards is best. In other words, don't reward behaviors every time they happen, since this will lead to children only doing good things if they are sure they will be rewarded. Rewarding good behavior randomly and occasionally keeps the children trying harder just "in case" this turns out to be one of those times that gets rewarded. Also, be sure that all children get a chance to be rewarded, not just a select few. It is a good idea to remember the slogan, "Catch 'em being good," to allow rewards to be given to students who ordinarily don't get them.

Research also tells us that smiles, praise, and other social forms of encouragement are better for the establishment of self discipline than material rewards such as candy, stickers, and gum. Praise must be sincere. Children, even the very young, can spot fake praise every time. Perhaps this is because the younger the child is, the more likely he is to pick up on body language which may not be the same as the verbal message. And, of course, they interpret the body language to be the truth.

Praise must also be specific. An experience from my own parenting has made that very clear to me. Years ago, I had one child among my three children who was compliant and easy to manage, while her siblings tended to be somewhat rebellious or "in your face" in defiance about many issues. I would sometimes say to her, "Laura, you are such a joy to me," and she would always reply, "Oh, Mother, don't say that!" After learning the psychological principle that one should always use specific praise, not general praise, I decided to pursue with her what the reason had been for her replies. This was when she had grown into a young adult. In answer to my questioning, she said to me, "It seems like every time you said that to me it would be just after I had done something really sneaky to my brother or my sister. It made me feel just horrible to think that you thought I was so good!" As I reflected on that, I realized that when someone comes to me and tells me how much they admire me, etc., etc., it makes me very uncomfortable, too. I think, "If she only really knew me---I am so far short of what I should be!" I now realize that I should have said something specific to Laura regarding a behavior she had just exhibited. I could have said, "It was so thoughtful of you to do the dishes without even being asked to do them. Thank you." This would have been citing a particular act for which she could justly receive praise, not a "glittering generality" she didn't feel she deserved.

In the lower grades (about second grade and below), it is extremely effective to give praise and attention to the children who are behaving appropriately. Such statements as, "I really like the way Susie is following along in her book and ready to read at any time," or "Johnny is certainly in the 'listen and learn position' with his legs folded criss-cross, his hands in his lap, and his eyes on me," will cause many of the other children to immediately begin to do the praised behavior. They want praise, too, and as mentioned earlier it is important to give praise to all children, not just a select few. This technique may work as high as the fourth grade in some schools, but there comes a time when children begin to be embarrassed by public praise from the teacher. They are afraid of being taunted by the other children for being the "teacher's pet." It will be important for you to read your feedback when using this technique above the second grade, and plan your use of praise accordingly. It's important to realize, however, that children of every age still appreciate genuine praise. The older children just prefer it to be given privately. A quiet "thumbs up" when a good job has been done, encouraging words of praise written on a paper that has been handed in, or just a pat on the back and smile when circulating during seat work, will let the child know you are proud of his behavior.

There are educational experts who are very much against the use of praise, so I must admit that it can do damage if it is not used appropriately. Yet I am not ready to say that it should not be used at all. First of all, I think it is the best method of getting children to administer self-encouragement. If you have commented to a child on how much neater his paper is than previously, or even how well his margins are being kept straight, the child will continue to "replay those tapes" to himself by saying, "I'm getting neater with my papers all the time." On the other hand, if all you do is write a big "MESSY" across all his papers, he will tend to "replay those tapes," too, saying, "I am such a messy person." In either case, the child will tend to live up or down to these self-expectations, and thus it will turn into a self-fulfilling prophecy. To guard against the harmful use of praise, if you use praise be sure it is sincere, specific, given to ALL students, and designed to be repeated by the child to himself as an encouragement.

One problem that some educators have with the use of praise is that it can be used to "manipulate" the students. It is true that we are trying to shape behavior, but if it is in the best interest of the student, it seems to me that having an arsenal of techniques for shaping behavior is not bad, but good. If it is sincere, you have the student's best interest at heart, and it produces the desired classroom atmosphere of making learning go forward more smoothly, I feel these behavior-shaping techniques definitely should be used. This is an issue which you should consider carefully, considering the widely varying opinions of experts, and do what seems right to you for your own classroom.

These Teacher Control models also believe in the judicious use of punishment, although they may differ as to what is appropriate punishment and when to use it. One of the dangers of punishment is that it may tend to weaken that all-important love/respect relationship between teacher and child if not used very carefully. To use punishment carefully, it is important that the teacher reflect sadness, rather than anger, at the student's behavior. Instead of an attitude of, "Well, I knew it would be you to break the rule,"(which tends to end up in a self-fulfilling prophecy) try to (sincerely) demonstrate sadness at the inappropriate behavior, and make a statement (after talking with the child about methods of self control) similar to, "I'm sure you'll do better next time."

My husband was a principal in high school for many years, and for years after that we have met ex-students in cities across the country as well as in our own city who would rush up to him and say, "Mr. Artmann, you really busted my bottom back in ____," shaking his hand up and down and smiling as if he were their best friend! This may sound strange, but let me tell you my husband's method of using corporal punishment. First, the student had to verbalize what he had done to deserve the punishment. Then, he had a choice of detention hall or other punishments if he preferred. And, my husband did not administer corporal punishment to girls. He did, however, sometimes have the girl's mother come up and deliver such punishment to girls if that was desirable. When the boy chose corporal punishment, after telling him how many "swats" he had earned, my husband would have him bend over the desk for support, and apply the swats to the well-padded rear end with a paddle in a way to cause stinging, but not damage. He would then have the boy stand up and look him in the eye, shake his hand, and receive the following speech. "Now, you've paid your price; nobody's mad at you. Go back to class and I don't want to see you in this spot again!" (Remember, Jesus said, "Neither do I condemn you; go and sin no more." John 8:11) And, true to his word, my husband would meet these students later in the hall with a big smile and a handshake, showing that he truly did not hold a grudge against them—they had paid for their misbehavior and had a fresh start. Perhaps that is one of the key problems with teacher–student relationships after misbehavior occurs. Whether punishment is used or not, it's important to offer the student a clean slate and expect the best of him. Many teachers simply do not allow this to happen.

A weakness of the use of punishment without counseling toward better behavior is the fact that sometimes the behavior will go underground. The student will learn to be more skillful at not getting caught, not at changing to a new behavior. Thus, even though you give the student a second chance, he must realize that you love him too much to allow him to continue in inappropriate behavior, for it will cause habit patterns that will not be in his best interest later in life. One of the pastors in our church made a statement one day that I thought was so profound that I wrote it in my Bible. He said, "Aren't you glad that God loves you just the way you are? But aren't you glad, too, that He loves you too much just to leave you that way?" As usual, our Lord has given us an excellent role model to follow. In our dealings with children, we should strive to act in the manner He deals with us.

A Plan for Misbehavior

Now in spite of all the careful planning, explanation of expectations, and judicious building of relationships, undesirable behavior will occur (although not nearly as often as if you had not done those things). At the risk of giving "cookbook instructions," which cannot be counted on to be successful since every situation and every child will be different, I want to run through some suggestions and a sequence which could be used. At times, you may want to skip over certain steps because of the severity of the infraction or the age of the children, but this suggested sequence will hopefully prove useful to you.

When you are in the middle of a lesson, try to ignore the behavior if it is not too obvious, or simply walk to the part of the room where the difficulty is starting to develop. This proximity control sometimes will allow you to proceed smoothly with the lesson without interruption. Even if you have to interrupt and give a corrective statement, try to do it in as low-key manner as possible. Many times children will misbehave because they get lots of attention by doing so. When you respond by giving attention, even though it is negative attention, the result is accidental positive reinforcement for the offending child. Your correction, therefore, should bestow as little attention as possible on the offender. Remember to give lots of attention to those children who are behaving appropriately. And especially remember to give lots of attention for the right reasons to the child who constantly misbehaves in an attempt to get your attention. But do it when he is behaving appropriately; remember, "Catch 'em being good!"

If the above plan is ineffective, go quietly and directly to the child and talk briefly with him. If this has failed in the past, or if you prefer, during the lesson quietly but firmly speak the child's name and give brief directions: "Susie, turn around. Your science book should be open to page 63, and you should be following along with the reading."

If the misbehavior continues, first excuse yourself to the class for having to interrupt the lesson ("Boys and girls, I am so sorry to have to interrupt our story, but we can't continue with it until this interference has been settled."), and then walk calmly and deliberately to the problem area. Gently place your hand on the child's shoulder and stoop down so that you are on eye level with him. When you have achieved total eye contact, talk quietly but firmly about expected behavior. If there are escalating problems, especially if anything disrespectful is said, remove the child to a private place (perhaps in the hall), giving the rest of the class an assignment to do while you are involved in settling the matter. This has two purposes. First, it allows you to preserve the offending child's dignity by questioning him at length about the behavior and allowing him to make any excuses he wants to make without the others listening to determine whether these excuses will relieve him from responsibility. Second, it leaves everybody wondering whether you will punish him severely. Some will hope you will; others will hope you won't. In either event, it has a sobering effect on the other children which will usually settle them back into their work. Thus a private conversation will allow you to be merciful or punitive, whichever you feel the situation demands. The other students tend to be deterred from similar behavior, as they watch you remove him with a stern look on your face.

A private talk with the child involves the child in thinking and talking about what has been done. It also helps him develop increased responsibility for his actions. Some suggestions of questions for this talk follow. You may, of course, vary them if they are inappropriate for the situation. Every situation is different. However, one thing holds true in all situations. Be sure to criticize the behavior, not the child himself. Try to aim toward an overall feeling that, "You are too fine a boy to act this way. I'm sure it's not the kind of behavior that you want people to think about when they hear your name."

First, ask the child, "What did you do?" Don't settle for **why** he did it, or ask him why. You'll probably get such things as, "He had it coming." "Johnny kept pestering me." or some other effort to involve others. You are only interested in getting him to verbalize what he, himself, did that was unacceptable. We are striving to help our children realize that the only behavior they can truly control is their own. How few adults recognize this! We have to move forward from other people's behavior and determine what our response will be to the behavior. That is our only true choice.

Secondly, ask him, "What makes this a problem?" This may seem like a very easy question, but we are trying to get the child to recognize that a) we cannot have an effective teaching/learning situation when there are noises and distractions, b)others have needs and feelings just like our own, and we should respect them, and/or c) he must respect the property rights of others just as he would have us to respect his.

Third, ask the child what he thinks should be done now. Be careful about requiring him to tell the other child, the class, or yourself that he is sorry. Every effort should be made to help him see how the other child or the class or the teacher feels, but if he is not sorry it is compounding the problem by making him lie because he is required to express that he is. All Christian disciplinarians do not agree concerning this, but I feel strongly about this matter and want you to think carefully about it before requiring insincere apologies. Allow an apology, public or private, if the child agrees that is the best course of action. However, in many cases, that is not enough, in which case you should offer the following question.

"How would that help?" Even a sincere apology does not erase the misdeed. If there has been destruction of property, some type of restoration is due. Help the child work through what would be an appropriate remedial action, and be sure to follow through to see that it is done. If parents need to be contacted, ask the child to tell his parents what has happened when he gets home, and to expect his teacher to call later. This gives him a chance to "break the news" before you call, yet does not allow him to believe that if he does not tell his parents they will never know.

Finally, whether or not the above question is needed, ask the child, "How could you handle this situation better next time?" It is important for him to realize that such situations occur over and over in life, and he should not get into a habit of responding inappropriately. Get him to walk through the situation verbally and tell you what he could do differently next time. And, the next time you see him stop to think in a similar situation and respond the right way, take the time to tell him how proud you are of how mature he is becoming! This is appropriate for any age of child. From kindergarten to college, all young people want to be recognized for showing mature behavior above and beyond the average for their age

If you feel that there should be consequences for the misbehavior in addition to counseling the child in a private talk, there are certain rules to keep on mind. First, start with demonstrating sadness, not anger, that you are having to assess a punishment so that it will help him to remember not to do this again. I personally would not use punishment for a first offense of this nature. However, when behavior has been repeated after warnings, it is important to not let it become habitual behavior.

Second, the consequences should be reasonable. Beginning teachers sometimes "use cannons to control little sparrows," as I have heard. Think of something that isn't too extreme. First of all, it will break the bond of teacher/student love and respect, and secondly it may be extremely hard to carry out without a great deal of difficulty.

Third, the consequence should be logical and relevant to the offense. One discipline program toward the middle of the disciplinary spectrum is based on a book called *Logical Consequences* . The man who wrote this book basically says that your consequence should be most like what would be a natural consequence. For example, if a child is going to run into the street, you couldn't give him the consequence of allowing a car to hit him, so then you make a **logical** consequence rather than a **natural** consequence. Perhaps he will not be allowed to play in the front yard for a period of time (a day or two can seem a long time to a preschooler), even with mom and dad present. Then, when he is brought out to the yard, he should be asked what he needs to remember about playing in the front yard. When he can verbalize that he should not go out into the street because a car might hit him, he should be allowed to play, with careful parental supervision. Similarly, a child who continually hits other children may have to be removed from playing with others until he can tell you that he has learned to play without hitting.

Fourth, the consequence should be private between you and the child. If he wants to tell others, fine. But you should respect his dignity by not telling the class what agreement has been made between yourself and him. That is one way you treat each child with respect.

Keeping in mind that the consequence should be logical and should help the child remember not to repeat the offense, there are several possible options to consider. The child may lose related privileges, such as not playing with other children for a time if he is treating them disrespectfully. If you have a team-related discipline approach, where the group helps each other to remember good behavior in order to competitively accumulate points for being "team of the week" or something like that, the child's team may lose points. This applies peer pressure to him, which can be cruel, so use it carefully and when gentler approaches have failed, if you choose to use it. The time-out chair is effective for grades K - 2, but only if it becomes a "thinking chair." The child is required to sit in the time-out chair only until he can come tell the teacher what he did wrong and how his behavior will change. Then he is allowed to return to the group, but returned to the chair to think some more if his behavior does not change. Too many times, a time-out chair becomes a way to get rid of the offending child so the teacher doesn't have to worry about him! That, of course, defeats the whole purpose of the chair, which is to help the child realize how his behavior must change for his own benefit. An older child could be required to write an essay about why this behavior is not acceptable, and why it isn't in his own best interest to act this way. You may get some deep, philosophical answers to this that could surprise you, or you may get, "Because the teacher will make you write an essay." Either one should be accepted, but the latter answer should give you an opportunity to ask the child verbally if he can think of any other reason, and then lead him to think of others.

Finally, if all else fails, take the child to a principal or outside counselor. However, never do this as a first consideration. You have been hired by the school to control your own classroom except in rare instances of needed outside intervention, and will find that sending too many children to the office gives you the reputation of a teacher who is not as "in control" as she should be.

Specific Behavior Problems

There are times when a specific type of behavior problem may call for a more individualized approach in addition to the generalized plan for misbehaviors that has already been given. When you understand the underlying cause of the misbehavior, that will give you the best key to how to deal with it. Although there are many other specific reasons for misbehavior than will be addressed here, I'll try to give some advice about a few common ones.

The Defiant Child

Some children will demonstrate from the beginning that their chief motivation is to be "in your face," expressing that they will not submit to your authority. In those cases, it is especially important to take strong action early. Defiance is sin, related to Satan's defiance when he said, "I will be like the Most High God." (Isa. 14:14) Strong wills must learn submission to authority early.

It is essential that you demonstrate strength with these children, both in your voice and in your body language, for their chief method is to invoke fear or weakness by their actions. And, by the way, they usually will despise you if you appear to them to be weak. Be strong, firm, calm, and controlled, ready to require obedience. After earlier methods have resulted in continued defiance, a possible verbalization with the child might be as follows. "I can see that you have some God-given skills that could make you a leader as an adult. God may call you to leadership someday. It is important that you first learn how to follow, for all great leaders must first learn this. God has placed me in charge of this classroom, and the Bible says we must come under the authority of those He has placed in authority. (Hebrews 13:17, 1Timothy 2:1-3). I am going to be strict with you, because I want you to grow to be a godly leader that God can use in His army." Children respond positively when they realize that we want to work **with** them for their best development because we care.

With younger children like this who refuse to do a required action, place your body firmly around theirs and literally "do it" with them. The time-out chair for thinking is also effective with the K-2 levels. At all levels, eye contact should be made while saying, "This is unacceptable. I will not allow you to act in this way. Do you understand me?"

Various Disruptions to the Lesson

The **talker** often isn't defiant, but just loves to talk. Stop the lesson, achieve eye contact, and gently remind him, perhaps with humor. This will be after having talked with him concerning "now it's my turn to talk" and "I'll respect you when it's your time to talk."

The **toucher** needs to touch something in order to feel "in contact." Get something into his hands to touch. Help him to be constructive with his touching, and remind him to respect other people's boundaries.

The **doer** learns best when movement is felt in the muscle-tone of his body. Therefore, if you keep him sitting too long, you cause problems for yourself as well as for him. Remember to vary the activity level of your lessons in order to help this child to cooperate and be successful. You may also have him "help you" by running errands for you within the classroom.

A **generally noisy class** must not be "talked over." The louder you get, the louder they will get. Also, you will be modeling loudness as acceptable. Flick a light, ring a bell, or use some other signal that you have taught them means silence. A game may also be used of holding up one hand as a hand signal. As children see you, the game tells them to "freeze," holding their hand up in the same way, until all have noticed and become quiet. Then you can praise the ones who first saw you, and thank all for cooperating. At this point, you need to remind them of why we cannot have class when it is too noisy (nobody can hear the lesson or directions), and how our noise is disturbing to other classes.

Friends talking during the lesson call for a calling out of their names and a reminder that this is not the time for visiting. If this is occurring while seat work is being done, in order to avoid disturbing the rest of the class, go to them quietly and tell them to "Hush." If such behavior continues on successive days, warn them that you will have to separate them if it continues, and at the next occurrence permanently change their seats (while demonstrating sadness at having to do this).

Hands raised during the teaching can be a special problem, because you always want to be sure to answer questions. Yet at times this interrupts the flow of the lesson or story. In such cases, say, "I really want to hear what you have to say, so I'll answer your questions and have you share in just a minute. But let's finish the story now."

Behavior Management in a Nutshell

In summary, never forget that your purpose in having an organized, attentive classroom is for the good of your students, so that they can learn academically and also learn to practice self control. It should never be allowed to turn into a personal desire for power or a vendetta against students that have been disrespectful to you. When you see your attitude changing to a defensive one toward certain students, let this be a matter of prayer, as you ask God to reveal to you what has gone wrong. Then ask Him to let you feel His love for these troublesome students, along with His plan for your classroom. This prayer has been known to result in a "problem" student touching the heart of the teacher until he actually becomes a "favorite." Sometimes, when we see these students as God sees them, and know what has gone into making them what they are, our hearts melt. When I was in training, I worked with a class that had an incorrigible little girl about eight years old who seemed to think tormenting the teacher was her favorite sport. We were allowed, as educational learners, to read the children's personal files. When I learned that she had already been sexually abused by a number of her family members, my attitude toward her changed completely. If we could see our children's backgrounds and current situations, sometimes we would come to realize that they are doing well to function as well as they do! A good adage to remember, with both students and fellow teachers, is "Be kind to everyone you meet, for all are carrying some kind of burden."

CHAPTER XIV

Putting It All Together

"And we know that all things work together for good to those who love God, to those who are called according to His purpose." Romans 8:28

Teaching is indeed a multi-faceted profession. It is both a science and an art. It is a science in that it has many specific principles and techniques which can cause a teacher to be more effective. I have endeavored to mention some of these in the preceding chapters. However, it is also an art, because there is much of intuition concerning specific children and situations which cannot be learned in advance, but must come from the heart. Both the science and the art are essential to the profession of teaching. It is foolish not to avail oneself of principles which have been proved workable through experience, yet it is equally foolish to believe that these principles operate in a "cookbook" method in every case.

The preparation of teachers has varied throughout the ages. Many have stated that if a teacher knows her subject matter, that is all that is necessary. However, most of us can testify of teachers who were very knowledgeable in their subject field but could not seem to put that knowledge into words comprehensible to their students. Or perhaps many of us could also tell of teachers who alienated their students to the extent that the students would not accept anything that they had to say. This latter dimension speaks of the art of teaching, which is something that comes from the soul, and perhaps surpasses the science of teaching in importance. Techniques and principles can always be learned, but if the soul of the teacher is not prepared correctly, she will not have the wisdom to search for the need in each individual situation and respond appropriately.

Maria Montessori was a highly respected teacher of young children in the early 20th century in Italy, and her methods are still used in various forms in many countries today. She was educated as a doctor, but since she was a woman, she was only able to be hired by a hospital for retarded children. It was through this situation that she developed her method of teaching. She received much fame because she was able to teach these retarded children well enough that they passed the Italian literacy test, which many normal Italian school children were never able to pass. She was also a devout Christian. I tell you this background on her in order to explain what was her philosophy on how to train teachers.

Montessori had a general statement about the training of teachers that, while it is over simplified, exemplifies much that current training of teachers may omit, and I would like to share it with you. She, of course, taught herself to teach, as she was trained as a physician. Since she was a scientist and a devout Christian, she felt that these were the characteristics that led her to understand teaching. She said that if she could instill in each future teacher the observational method of the scientist and the compassionate heart of the dedicated Christian, she would then send that future teacher to the children, and from the children she would learn to teach. Let that sink in for a minute. It is a great concept on which to meditate. No matter how much training you have, there are always going to be times when your observation of a particular child and/or a particular situation, coupled with your love for that child or those children, will show you what you should do. And, if what is shown is that you should bring it to your Father in Heaven in prayer, that is perhaps the most valuable lesson of all.

"...What is that in your hand ?"

There is just one other thought that I would like to leave with you. When God told Moses to go to Pharaoh asking for the release of the Hebrews from bondage, Moses was afraid and felt very inadequate. Do you remember what God said to him? He said, "What is that in your hand?" (Ex.4:2)

He then proceeded to show Moses all the things that He, God, could do with the ordinary rod that Moses held in his hands. He could turn it into a snake and back into a rod if Moses would only obey Him. The rod was what Moses used to earn his living–the simple rod of a shepherd. God can take the simple talents and training our students have and turn them into great tools for His purposes. As teachers, it is our responsibility to see that they have these simple, foundational tools, like the shepherd's rod, for the Master's use. Reading, writing, and arithmetic are just such tools. What an awesome responsibility it is to be a teacher! But, thanks be to God, we don't have to do it in our own strength and wisdom!

If you have been called to be a teacher, He says to you, "What is that in your hand? What talents and background have I already given to you? If you will give them to me, I will turn them into everything you need to be the teacher I have called you to be."

And now the limited wisdom of this book is coming to an end. I have tried to share with you the science and the art of teaching that I have both studied and utilized over the past 35 years, and it is my prayer that these will be of use to you. However, all the books that have been written or may be written in the future could never contain all the things that you might find useful. It is now time for you to go forward, with God's hand in yours, and be the blessing that God has called you to be in the lives of His children. You will have talents and intuitions that I never dreamed of having. God uses all of His children differently, and I pray that you will be all that He has called you to be.

When I began my teaching career at the Christian university where I taught for 28 years, the dean gave a devotional that was particularly meaningful to me because I was, to tell you the truth, afraid that I was not sufficient for the task that lay before me. The theme of that devotional is summed up in Joshua 1:9, where it says, "Have I not commanded you? Be strong and of good courage; do not be afraid nor be dismayed, for the Lord your God is with you wherever you go." I can truly testify that He has indeed been with me, and I commit to you that He will be with you, as well!

"Not that we are sufficient of ourselves to claim anything as coming from ourselves; our sufficiency is from God..." II Corinthians 3:5

CPSIA information can be obtained at www.ICGtesting.com
Printed in the USA
LVOW040347140412

277567LV00002B/5/P